The Stolen House of Light

a novel by

Susan Estall

Fre Sally Enjoy the story & the history

River Pearl Press
Hawaii, Illinois

Susan Estall Feb. 8, 2010

First printing 2009
Printed with soy ink on recycled paper

ISBN 9780982048825
LCCN 2009903529

ATTENTION, UNIVERSITIES, COLLEGES, PROFESSIONAL ORGANIZATIONS, and CORPORATIONS: Quantity discounts are available on bulk purchases of this book for educational, gift purposes, or as premiums for increasing magazine subscriptions or renewals. Special books or book excerpts can also be created to fit specific needs. For information, please contact River Pearl Press, 44 Ogden Avenue, Downers Grove, IL 60515; or River Pearl Press, 3200-C Wawae Road, Kalaheo, HI 96741; or visit www.thestolenhouseoflight.com.

Author's note: Stories about George Hunley are family stories. Preservation research is courtesy of Downers Grove Library reference librarians. Sections of historical stories are courtesy of Downers Grove Park District Museum. Hibbing house moving research is courtesy of Hibbing Historical Society.

Dedicated to my husband, Marty
our beloved daughter, Julianna
my mother and grandmother
our house mover, E. Hyatt
& my friend, Shobhana.

Acknowledgments

My deep gratitude is extended to the caring people who shared their kindness as I walked my life's journey and writer's path. To my friends, to my readers, and to people I will always remember: The Kamani family, E. Hyatt, Mildred and Donald Drew, Al and Glennette Tilley Turner, Susan Campbell, Leatrice Shay, Dale Taylor Micek, Dr. Ruth Hoffman, Linda Schlais, Chris, Jennifer, Julia, and Elizabeth Kahlke, Kathy Werler, James Werler, Dr. Edward Cho, Christopher Jones, Dr. Dorothy May, Jean Jung-McBride, Zakia Aziz, Ivy and Evo, Deanna Teel, Connie Teel Oleson, Jan Biesner, John LaPorta, Dr. Daksha Mehta and Aalap Mehta, Dennis Hightower, Holly Saunders, Sue Glanz, Mr. Spanogal, Freya Secrest, Katy McDonough, The Richard family, M. Jakubowski, Kenny Wainwright, Michael Shewmaker, Mary Martin, Lynn and Jeff Fields, Mike, Kim, and daughters Taylor, Lindsay, and Sarah Grace Born, Robin Laws, Jamie Lee Silver, Catherine Leyden, Duchie Kuntz, Caroline and Don Stanhope, Christopher L. Richards, Mary Wade, Greg Mansfield and Kerby Hogge, Christine Myles, Ann Springer, Diane and Pat Dailey, Kate Skegg, Nora and Chris Blackaller, The Salmans, David and Kimberly Thompson with daughters Manon and Cosette, Hillary Frances, The Williams, The Tumeas, The Mikolajzaks, The Spriets, The Schultzs, Mrs. Chynoweth, Don and Eunice Schatz at: The Urban Life Center, Penny Berry,

Emily Scharf, Robin and Robert Vance, Judy Balian, Diane Forkin, Ali Yazdi, Gerri and Erin Korzen, The Boland family, The Sikdar family, Madeline Altman, John Stehura, and several groups: Friends in Questers, Blodgett Legacy Partnership's enthusiastic board: Chris Jones, Sally Remmington, Anne Miller, Shirley Hiddleston, with additional thanks to John Hiddleston; Potawatomi Caravan friends: Susan Campbell, George and Pat Godfrey, Wayne and Therese McNary, Eddie Joe Mitchell, Virginia, Janet, and Bob Pearl, Thomas and Marshall Wabnum, Shirley and Bill Willard; and last but not least: our special friends from Aix-en-Provence, France: Nobert Lopez, Delphine Lopez and family, and Pascal Metzinger and family.

I wish to acknowledge professors and universities for fond memories: University of Illinois at Springfield or formerly Sangamon State University: Dr. Carol Fee Ivanoff, Dr. Cullom Davis, Margaret Rossiter, Dr. Larry Shiner, Wilma Scott Heide; University of Illinois at Chicago: Dr. Harriet Wadeson, Dr. Pat Allen; University of Southern California: Dr. Estel Andujo, Dr. Lubin; Haskell Indian Nations University: Dr. George Godfrey; Governor State University: Dr. Rev. Larry McClellan; and from Dhaka, Bangladesh: "Chacha" an unforgettable English literature professor.

To colleagues and professionals I respect and offer my gratitude: Dan Lippmann, Linda Metzger, Mythili Jaganath: all three of you will always have a special place in my heart; to Harry Harrison, Dr. Carolyn Lund Dennis, Dr. Cho, Mary Martin, Dr. Das, Dr. Sheppard, Stephanie Bien, Susan Hurwich, and Julianne Walker: thank you for being a part of my life's journey. I wish to extend my deep respect to former clients for their courage. I also wish to thank John Lowe for his spirit of community, architect Mike Jackson for his research, Tom Sisul and Sue Fors for generous assistance, Dr.

MaryBeth Webeler for her warmth, Ginny Lauterbach for the twinkle in her eye, Jodie Eilers for being a teacher extraordinaire, and Mr. Oda for his enthusiasm.

To those who have inspired me with their creativity and written work: Jhumpa Lahiri for her exquisite writing: *The Interpreter of Maladies;* James W. Fowler for his developmental model of spirituality: *The Stages of Faith;* Julia Cameron for her unfailing support of writers: *The Right to Write* and *The Artist's Way;* Stephanie Pace Marshall for new learning models: *The Power to Transform;* J. Ruth Gendler for word images: *The Book of Qualities;* Glennette Tilley Turner for her thirty years of research: *The Underground Railroad in Illinois* and *An Apple for Harriet Tubman;* Sidney M. Jourard for the quest for authenticity: *The Transparent Self;* Arundhati Roy for her words about nature: *The God of Small Things;* Azar Nafisi for her insight: *Reading Lolita in Teheran;* Nathanial Hawthorne for a first American heroine: *The Scarlet Letter;* Fritjo Capra and his ideas of shifting from an industrial age to a solar age: 1983 Washington, D.C. conference; David Spangler for his depth: *Parent as Mystic, Mystic as Parent;* Helen Harris Pearlman for an early loved book: *Relationship;* Mary-Elaine Jacobson for her work: *The Gifted Adult;* Dolores Curran for a vital focus: *Traits of a Healthy Family;* Karen Hesse for my daughter's favorite: *The Aleutian Sparrow;* Melvin Morse for understanding children: *Closer to the Light;* Susan Campbell and Shirley Willard for devotion: *The Potawatomi Trail of Death: 1838 Removal from Indiana to Kansas;* Andre DuBus III for writing in his car: *The House of Sand and Fog;* Jack Weatherford for his expansive work: *Indian Givers;* Judy Chicago for women in history: *The Dinner Party;* Paul Reiser for his series that made me laugh: *Mad About You;* writers for two favorite films: *Grey Owl* and *Made in Heaven,* Vonda McIntyre for a fictional healer: *Dreamsnake;* Abigail Thomas for her gems: *Thinking About Memoir;* and Robert Henri on art and creativity: *The Art Spirit.*

A special acknowledgment and thank you for help from my editor, Sue Collier, whose even temperament, caring, and guidance helped me to stay the course and write a better book; Laura Fortin for her creativity and clever design skills; Shobhana Kamani for thirty years of friendship; Meghan Kamani for her centeredness; Susan Campbell for pearls; Glennette Tilley Turner for adventures; Leatrice Shay for sharing and conversations; Dale Taylor Micek for enthusiastic support, and Millie Drew for caring.

I thank my dear family: especially my husband, Martin Estall and daughter, Julianna Estall, for their continual support of this book; thanks to our special Indiana Branch: Bill and Kathy Werler (you believed in my book); Rich, Carolyn, Megan, and Madison Broyles; Tom, Nate, and Christopher Werler; Swedish Branch: Anna and Christopher L. Werler; Illinois Branch: Dorothy Werler (you always had faith in me); Jim & Betty (and their two terrific daughters) Jamie and Kristin Werler; Judy Schubach, Dick Massey and families (thanks for the suitcase full of family photos); Bob and Marie Galbraith, Linda and Susan Galbraith; Texas Branch: Grace Van Berg, Dan, Marsha, Diane and Susan Morrison (thanks for the stories); Oregon Branch: The Wolfs; Florida Branch: Vera Watson, Seattle Branch: Linda Schlais (a special Aunt), Andrew, Cheryl, and Jayme Schlais; English Branch (a family of travelers): Leslie and Audrey Estall, Lorraine, Peter, and Alexander Smith; Natasha, and Nigel, and Dylan Bishop; Sara and Wayne Shipley; Michael, Tracey, Charolette and Gregory Estall; and Fredrick Estall of Wales. To my father, Frank Werler, and to Verner Wolf, Grant Dickie, and Johnathan Fields: all four of you left this earth sooner than anyone wanted. Lastly, to my remarkable grandmother, Dorothy Lee Hunley Wolf Beyer and to my ancestors, who live on in memory: I hope to honor you with this book.

Susan Estall

Seeds

Ever since they blew dandelion seeds out back, when summers were long and full of the wind, Sarah and Linnea had been good and gentle friends. They would sit with soft piles of plucked stems and blow when the wind was strong, which was often because of the silvery green lake and stone bluffs nearby, with air currents honed for plant spreading. Silky seeds would slowly float up after the girl's heavy wet breath freed those little umbrellas of circumstance.

The girls were spell-bound by the seeds' airborne sense of timelessness. They would gaze silently at their seeds floating on sunny days when eternity filtered into summer. Seeds soft and lightly transparent held their focus and gave a quiet grace to those childhood days. In the sharing of the stillness in nature, they knew a unity of worlds, a heaven and earth blended. It was in that graceful sphere of time suspended that a sweet friendship between Linnea and Sarah was determined. Blessed with a transcendent bond between them, they became soul-linked with silky seeds, moist breath, and the quiet of early, warm summer days.

Linnea's small stone house was set near a cliff. Over the edge were the bluffs carved from ancient glaciers, which also left the gift of the Mississippi due west of their flagstone home. Winds would gush by, giving Linnea's mother the fear of God that one of the girls would get too near the edge. But Linnea didn't need to listen to the warnings, as she was a level-headed child and stayed back. But Sarah—she was another story. Yet somehow the wind always came to her aid, as if a spell cast upon that invisible force kept her protected, as irrational as most knew that to be. Wind, that is, as protection from a cliff.

Sarah thought of God as not being all made up of worry, and she frowned at her auntie's words, "You'll put the fear of God in me." Sarah knew deeply from many a night outdoors, homeless and alone with her mother, at least three things about God. She knew God was the blessing that gave stars their glimmer. She knew God was as flexible as the wind. And Sarah knew God had put her right there behind that small stone house, with a distant "cousin" and a family willing to embrace her innocent heart and sweep her into the goodness of their own.

Sarah was a distant relative who had come to stay for awhile with Linnea and her parents. That "awhile" turned into the rest of her childhood, as her birth mother remained homeless and unable to care for her. Not comprehending the circumstances of Sarah's mother's illness, the girls thought it brilliant for them to be together. They took each day as it came and seldom did they look back, except Sarah, who on quiet nights remembered her mother's almost warm hand in hers, their breath making disappearing white mist as they walked in the cold. She could still feel the chill and the warmth in some distant memory held within her own smooth skin. In those somber moments, Sarah knew she had a mother who was apart from her, and she knew she had a longing.

When Sarah and Linnea were nine years old, and destiny had brought the two together, they became inseparable, like two peas in a pod: green, fresh, crisp, and bursting. If not dampened by situation, their energy level was exuberant, with Linnea being the one full of schemes and Sarah the reflective participant. Together they were a force of creative living, bound only by their childhood imagination, and perhaps a few adult and worldly restrictions. As complimentary twins they knew a bond discovered rarely in a lifetime. It was the friendship of souls, united in fantasy, with a closeness echoed in the joys of nature shared.

Dandelion seeds turned out to be their happy, if solemn, pastime. Sarah was the one who wondered where the seeds would end up. As she lightly blew apart the spheres, she asked, "Where do they go, all these seeds?" Linnea just listened and watched.

Sarah wondered if another golden flower might grow, or if the seed would get crushed and be forever left destitute, without a chance to flourish. Sarah was the philosopher, who pondered. Linnea was the one whose father said, "You'll figure out how to get the darn things to grow." Sarah and Linnea were probably the only two human beings who ever planted dandelion seeds in pots, and waited and watched.

Once they had a contest to see which girl could get the seed to sprout first. Linnea did her research at the small, local library with the scent of old books that brought back memories of her gracious grandmother, the painter of wild roses, who had her own botanical history. Linnea checked out numerous books, reading up on seedlings and on the tenacious dandelion with its more than stubborn root. Then she planned her experiment well — so she thought.

Sarah, on the other hand, was more for creating rituals, being the child who walked with the mystery in each day. With green pond water and honeysuckle potions and crooked stick wands she was ready to compete. She did her magic on her spot of earth in a pot, and then put it in a dark closet for germination, for too many days.

Neither ritual nor research gave many results, but the girls laughed out loud at the dormant seeds. They then stood staring at those seeds: ill in Sarah's pot and only a bit less sad in Linnea's. They said it was competitiveness that caused them to fail their seedlings — and themselves. They sensed even then that competition could be their downfall as friends. From that day forward they vowed they would never again compete with one another.

2

The Imaginary House

Sarah's fantasy of a house started early. Maybe it was because of the gypsy life she had led with her mother for too long. She always knew her mother was different, but she could wrap herself around that reality quite well, like a thick vine circling the rough, beautiful texture of a tree. Her mother was a "willow"...wispy, changeable as the wind, with a charm of her own. "See that tree over there? It knows some things we don't," her mother would tell her. Sarah remembered looking intently at the old sycamore tree and thought maybe it knew about its roots.

Sarah knew her mother saw the world through different eyes, and so did she. As an innocent thrown into the reality of adult pain too early, she quickly learned to maintain keen perceptions. Some kept her safe, some helped her to see the world with more curves than angles and that was the blessing of her mother, even if she was unable to finish raising her.

Images of houses came to Sarah's mind during those tender years between six and nine, when she was homeless and half dreaming. Or at times she would awaken, startled by the suddenness of daylight, and need an escape from the homeless fate she lived. Houses would come to her imagination, and one evolved into a whole fantasy where she lived, at least in the freedom of her own mind.

If reality became too uncomfortable on a cold night, she would slip into her "house" with its fireplace, which in her way of thinking seemed to keep her cozy and warm. Like a Himalayan sherpa who knew how to use a focused mind to keep warm, she could do the same. While Sarah wandered homeless with her mother in California or Oregon, it was the winter months of rain that were especially cold and damp. To cope on those coldest nights she became a child lost in a pretend world, envisioning herself with her mother in their fantasy house, a home that stayed as warm as needed. It was always a perfect temperature.

Pink roses were planted across the front of the house, and at both sides of the door. She could see them in bloom; even smell their sweetness whenever she needed to forget the sickening, too sweet smell of alcohol on one of her mother's travel companions. The greater her need to escape, the more pungent the smell of her pale pink roses. She could breathe in her imaginary scent, to fill her small lungs for a good while, full of that mix of earth and heaven called rose.

The house evolved into a soft sky-blue color, with the door set in the center of the house front, and that was a must. Equal windows on both sides gave Sarah the equilibrium that had been refused her because of her lack of a home. Her mind comforted her in this way, allowing some balance in an unbalanced world of growing up.

Life had not always been such. Her first five years were quite different when her father was living and her mother happier and not yet a victim of her history and heritage. Sarah recalled her handsome father, a man of East Indian descent, telling stories and laughing as fully as any man could. She remembered she loved hearing his resounding laughter as she intently watched the movement of his facial expressions when they sat cherishing those stolen moments together.

"Sarah, come listen to my story about the Bengal tiger—a regal animal and a tricky one," he would tell her. Other evenings he would sit with her on his lap and describe the lush green land where he was born. Sarah could envision rivers from the world's highest mountains filtering down to nourish the tropical foliage of the delta region where her father grew up.

That was before his drowning in the pool by their ocean side apartment. That was before the tragedy that suddenly grasped her father from her and she knew grief unfortunate for a child. That was before her mother had no one to help because her family of origin abandoned her when she married outside her race. It was before her mother's thinking became soft, before the days of a heavy, homeless, misplaced future.

Sarah had learned her love of images from her father who painted vivid ones in his stories, now infused in her memory. She especially loved pictures of houses and doors, and since her reading was cut short with her homeless living, images became all the more potent to her childlike mind. Sarah had once seen in a magazine a photo of a Dutch door, and it was such a curiosity to her child eyes. She thought she could open the bottom half of that door, to go in and out, and that made great sense to her as a little one. She saw herself moving back and forth through this Dutch door, and she had great fun with that imaginary, heather-colored split door. On the top half, she put in an oval window of multicolored glass with an image of one pale, peach-colored rose. One beautiful, fragile rose, a rose of eminent calm.

And when she really needed to leave the confines of her homeless days, she could become that single, glass rose. Her sense of her self would merge with her colored glass flower, and a stillness would come to her as if she were seeing loads of stars at night, which she did when on Arizona desert roads, away from city lights. Being swept up into the vastness of twinkling stars, or stilled into a rose of soft colors and curves, helped her to cope those four years of aimless wandering. Those were the years she held tight to her mother's hand. Her mother always knew where she was — except when Sarah was lost in her own imagination or her mother was lost inside her own mind.

Her ethereal house had shutters either side of all windows, because shutters meant security. A house with shutters meant somehow that family had arrived at a place of virtue. Calm was framed in those windows by white shutters set against blue walls — a cool, peaceful blue that would not be disturbed. Winter whites, powder blues, and soft flower pinks colored her imaginary home, which became more real to her than at times it should. But if her fantasy kept her from the hurt of not having a home, nor a living father or a consistent mother, so be it.

Sarah also had a specific memory, a stored image from when she and her mother went traveling on a bus, the free tickets the result of some county that wanted them both, in all their homelessness, to leave its boundaries. She was a small child, so no suspicions of a lack of schooling had yet been aroused. But she was not as young as she appeared, and for her age, she was wisely observant.

As she looked out her bus window, she was saddened as she watched houses flash by, their images reflected in and through glass, as if she were in a dream. She saw ethereal homes she expected would never exist in her future. She wondered how people managed to live there. What was their good fortune that gave them a home but not her? Their reality seemed as fluid as the unreality of her imagined home. A house she could touch, put a hand to brick or fingers to a door-knob in this world, was as much a dream to her as it was a tangible thing to those who lived in and owned one. She knew a house was out of reach, not accessible—an untidy longing. But in the images of her mind, and in its freedom, she could have exactly as she wanted.

3

Trust

It took Sarah some years to trust her husband enough to tell him of her childhood fantasy house from years ago. Not that he couldn't be trusted, because he could and he cared for her in a tender way as no one before knew how. Still, her images were part of her raw pain from her childhood past, and only slowly did she talk about either one.

"You know, Tyler, I have forgotten much of it. But I do remember the cold," she once told him.

When she spoke she felt a bit deafened, as if wind was blowing, but she knew that was her protective veil between adult life and childhood trauma. She knew it helped her to talk, and so she did, and Tyler listened at those moments without comment. He took in her words as if he were a sponge cleaning up a mess someone else had made. Her words of roses, shutters, and Dutch doors penetrated into him, into his muscles, as if stored there he could help carry the weight of her history.

"Tell me again about the house you dreamed up," he would ask her.

And it was as if Tyler could see the house in a dream world of his own. He could make out the soft blue clapboard walls and the pristine white shutters. He could see the flowering arbor covering a flagstone path to Sarah's heather-colored Dutch door. He could envision the roses at the house front and up the archway path, and he knew just which ones he would plant for her.

This was the first time fantasy and reality met, when Tyler knew he would purchase American Beauties, in pink. He preferred red roses and so would put them on the side of the house he fantasized one day building for her. He was gifted with his hands, able to craft and create with them, and he knew he had stored in the bones of his fingers the hope of the structure of that fantasy house.

Ty just wished it was not so far off in their future. They had started their small savings for a home, cash stuffed in a very large jar hidden in their rented kitchen, a space paid for on bartered time to their jobs. When it would reach enough money he never knew, as at times a hand went in the jar pulling out for their needs. But Sarah kept faithful deposits even if only a few dollars, because that was always more than she had as a homeless child, before Linnea and her parents opened their home and honored her as their own.

Tyler and Sarah had met in Havener, Illinois, where Sarah had come to live with Linnea's family. Havener was a small community in the western part of Illinois situated on a small river, its source the Mississippi River. It was a town full of old houses and with parks dotted by two-hundred-year-old oak trees. When she first met him Sarah had been in her favorite town park, called Ragsdale Park, and because her bike chain slipped off, Ty offered to help fix it. She was not used to having such offers and watched as Tyler's capable hands helped her to have wheels again. Sarah knew how to fix it herself, had many times, but she welcomed his efforts. As they spoke in their mild, shy Midwest manner, she learned he was a carpenter working at the fretwork factory in town.

"I have always wanted to know how to work wood with my hands. You know — how it feels to sand wood and make a finished piece," she told him.

"Well, if you call me I'll show you. I can teach you a lot about wood," he said with a faint smile.

She took him up on his offer, much to his surprise, and he was good for his word. Late at night he would sneak her into his day job work area and begin to teach her, which not only is how they came to know and care for one another, but it is also how their hands met and got to know one another. His were hands with slender fingers, like a pianist's hands but with the texture of a working man; hers were fuller palms with strong, long fingers and soft, silky skin. Their bodies first met through their hands, and their love would continue to be discovered with their hands — not only sensually, but through the integrity inherent in them.

Tyler also fell for her eyes, felt he was in motion when he found himself lost in the deep and glimmering green of those vulnerable spheres. Her skin, a blend of brown and cream, only accentuated the peridot of her eyes. Her short hair was tempered brown with snatches of gold that fell softly on her temples, like fine silken thread hinting at her history. She was all that was best between her mother and father, her body containing the blend of two cultures in a way only Sarah could unify, and with a mind just as penetrating as the intensity of her history.

When Tyler touched her hand, when he later looked hesitantly into her spring green eyes, when he heard her ideas, he knew they would marry. He knew without question he would listen to her stories, and he knew for all of his days he would love her. Two years later they were married, in a small house wedding at Linnea's family stone cottage, where Tyler vowed to Sarah he would listen to all her stories.

Ty was the kind of man who thought love was an action, so he was always doing for Sarah with his capable hands. He could feel but could not articulate her raw pain, and so he filled his fear of her sorrow with action. It did take many rough edges off her life, bringing round the curves that Sarah knew so well were part of things spiritual. "God has curved thoughts," she told herself more than once, and her Tyler helped to bring about more of that rounded reality, even if her philosophical underpinnings puzzled him.

Tyler perceived Sarah as thinking too much, but he had learned long ago from other women's dismay at the idea to not voice this opinion. So he kept this idea to himself, as frustrated as it left him at times. Besides, it would not change her way even if he did speak up, because Sarah was always thinking about something. He assumed the night stars of her childhood were the root cause, along with many homeless nights.

Those sad memories, of her less than perfect childhood and of her fantasy home, got him to thinking his own multiple thoughts about what she never had, what he knew she deserved, and what he was entitled to own but had not been able to make happen. He knew they needed a house, a home to embrace her and their small family so to repair the past. He understood viscerally Sarah's need for a sense of place she could finally call her own and he was near desperate to make it happen.

"Sarah, I want a house. I'm tired of living here," he repeated, frustrated. He felt hemmed in by their apartment and had trouble being at peace within its confining walls.

"Don't you think one day we will have a house?" she asked, assuming at least he could hold on to the vision for them both.

He doubted Sarah's assumption, but he did not

question his conviction that she needed that elusive but all powerful sense of place. He had known it himself, both in the steadfast home his parents had kept for their children and in his family history. Tyler's father was the genealogist of their roots and the stories he told Ty gave him a sense of belonging he had always taken for granted. Although he accepted it as a given, he realized Sarah was missing that sense of place. She was like a wanderer without a culture of her own or a sense of her unique history. She lacked that secure feeling of being from a particular home upon the earth, from a family linking her to a culture of strengths if also a culture of shortcomings — the paradox of all cultures.

As Tyler reviewed her needs, while sensing his own wants, he had such a desire for a solution. He wanted it sooner than later and the impatience growing inside him started to bereft him, if ever so slightly, of his integrity. He was willing to do whatever it would take to get Sarah a house and home. It would be worrisome for her if she knew his willingness to take the wrong risks.

As he became completely focused on a house as the answer to remedy all pain, he grew in his confidence in being able to provide one. He knew then, with his pride expanded to the rough perimeter beyond his honesty, someday he would "gift" her in the way he knew how to give. He would, on all accounts, with the hard-earned strength in his hands, help create for Sarah a house she would call home.

4

The Tangible House

Sarah and Linnea still lived in Havener, Illinois, where they had grown up together. The town was established in the mid-eighteen hundreds, and many old houses built there remained on those quiet, tree-lined avenues. Both women loved to walk the aged cobblestone streets while observing the old, majestic homes and stately trees, treasuring their time together at dusk. In winter Sarah said the dark tree branches looked like fine black lace up against the vibrant royal-blue sky. Then, in her softened voice, she would recite lines from one of her tree poems, whispering in the early dark, "calligraphy against the dusk sky, tree script in the night wind."

Their friendship was as strong and lively as ever, with goodwill passing back and forth as if they had a secret knowing about life. They met as often as they could, and when Linnea was not busy at the local newspaper, which her parents had struggled to purchase many years back, she would meet Sarah for a meal. They had late lunches in the park on warm, sun-filled days, or when Midwest weather was too stormy or cold, they would meet at their local hangout, where Sarah worked as a day-time waitress.

On this day, a rain-weary day, they sat in their booth for as long as they could spare and talked. By this time both women had married and they both had one child: Linnea had a daughter, Blair, and Sarah had her daughter, Julia.

"The girls are writing a play. Forget trying to interrupt them," said Sarah, smiling softly.

"I know; they're so focused," said Linnea. She was still surprised at the girls' ability to concentrate.

"I love listening to the sound of their voices when they play together. They have the same intensity we had," Sarah said.

"We still have that intensity, when we can find the time to get together. Do you realize the girls are about the same age now as when we first met?" added Linnea.

"And full of adventure, just like we were," Sarah said, recalling some of their history.

The girls, like their mothers, were also steadfast friends. Blair and Julia, who were always together, were like the wind, in constant movement, and so had to be monitored carefully, even if their nine years gave the girls some abilities to help them navigate their small village.

Time for both mothers was never as it had been, and in fact they had almost forgotten how it was different before they had birthed their daughters. It had been freer, but in a self-indulgent way that did not really become either woman. Children, while demanding, as both women knew, created a shift in healthy ways from being self-focused. Sarah and Linnea were not narcissistic or overly self-involved but were quite competent mothers, able to set aside their own needs and give. Yet they also knew they needed time for themselves and their friendship.

They knew their lunches together were a balm needed to restore their inner wells so they could keep giving to their children and to others. They guarded those times of shared friendship, woman to woman, like protecting a vein of gold found near a river bed: solid gold coursing through dark soil, fed by crystal river water, hidden unless one keeps on the search. When they gathered as women in friendship, built upon bedrock, that hour together could sustain their mothering for a good week. Again though, they would have to dive in for more and if several weeks passed without their shared sustenance both could get edgy, insisting to the other that they had to get together. They would then meet again, for their talks were soothing, but even more healing was the quiet way they could just be together, a silent knowing only good friends carry.

It was on this day, after a comforting silence, that Sarah heard Linnea's news. The latest town event was always a known to Linnea because working at a newspaper meant she often heard the new news first. But today's conversation surprised Sarah more than any previous talk. Maybe it was because Linnea was the more practical one that Sarah was caught off guard, but she was stunned by the assortment of feelings Linnea's good news brought up in her. Feelings of sorrow and longing and then small hints of jealousy, which she observed but did not feed because she knew such pangs came only from her own limited sense of what she could and could not have.

Linnea had been following the fate of an old house built before the American Civil War, which made the house nearly a century and a half old. Both women knew the old house from childhood as a well-worn feature on one of the prettiest tree-lined streets of their town. And that was the problem, because that smaller house did not hold up in the competition of the far grander houses on the block, and that quaint block was in demand.

"The Wolter's old house might be torn down," Linnea said, observing Sarah's reaction.

"Why their house? It's been around a long time," Sarah said, unhappy to hear the news.

"Their house goes back to eighteen-fifty-three. The plan is to demolish it to make way for one of the new, false stone houses," Linnea added.

"They try to make them look old when it's a facade," Sarah said. "Doesn't history mean anything to people?"

"Makes you wonder," Linnea said.

"And the Wolters are such nice people; I know they have to leave but I'm sorry to see them move away and their home torn down," said Sarah, who would miss visiting the older couple in their house.

"Their home is a decent old house, no doubt about it," Linnea said, nodding her head.

"I wish they weren't tearing down so many houses in our town," Sarah added.

"It's not just in our town where houses have come down. I've been researching newspaper articles on teardowns. It's a more complex environmental problem than you think, and it's happened all around the country," said Linnea.

"I've always loved old houses. They're usually so well built," Sarah said.

"They just don't make them today like they used to," Linnea added.

Linnea was aware that new houses, while having up-to-date floor plans, could not afford to be built from wood equal to that of the past. The wood of old homes had been better cured and was of better quality because it was from old growth forests. Linnea had done her research and discovered that some pre–Civil War houses in her area were even built from oak, while many other houses after the Civil War were built with white pine from northern Wisconsin.

That old wood, from trees sacrificed in old growth forests or groves, was well preserved, and the strength in it had endured. The two-by-fours actually measured two inches by four inches, unlike the cut wood of the day that measured one and one-half inches by three and one-half inches. The change in measurement was made in the early twentieth century to save wood, but the name "two-by-four" was never altered.

Linnea had compared the positives and negatives of both old and new houses. Although new houses had some aspects that fared better than older homes, such as energy efficient furnaces and air conditioners, she knew they were structurally not equal to older homes. Elements of energy efficiency, such as double-pane windows, were better in new homes, but custom-made storm windows put over old windows in rennovated homes was also a good option. She thought the better structure of an older home with thick plaster walls, which added to sound-proofing, was more to her liking. Besides, old houses had a certain charm with their beautiful trim work and nooks and crannies, which Linnea loved. She had noticed in her community that many of the new designs had the appearance of looking old, but they lacked genuineness. And to both women, they lacked history.

"Wasn't the Wolter's house part of the Underground Railroad?" Sarah asked.

"It was. My parents did a story about it before I started working at the paper," Linnea said.

The home in question, a house that would heal wounds of the past if it was given half a chance, was part of the Underground Railroad during the eighteen hundreds, when many black people escaping slavery were assisted on their road to freedom by both blacks and whites. People were hidden in houses, attics, cellars, barns, empty cisterns, even secret rooms — wherever they would not be caught — on their way to northern states and later to Canada. In that very house, with a beckoning history in its walls, many courageous people who risked their lives to escape the injustices of slavery, had been hidden until it was safer at night for them to travel further north.

The Underground Railroad was not a real railroad as some imagined. There was no underground tunnel for actual railroad cars. It was a secret trail of passage, from house to house, for the brave persons seeking freedom. Some used to say it was as if people disappeared underground, so it was called "the underground" with railroad added because trains held a fascination when they started to roar through the landscape. Sometimes people, white and black, traveled together on the Underground Railroad, with people escaping slavery hidden in wagons with false bottoms. Other times, those seeking freedom were on foot, finding their own way while hoping to discover those with the morality to care and the will to help.

Both women, who knew the house was part of the Underground Railroad, were not aware of the full significance of the house, or the vitality of the movement it represented, and of the monumental risks people took to escape slavery. They sat bemoaning the sad fate of other old houses they had seen torn down, and the possible bulldozing of the 1853 Underground Railroad house would be another great loss. As the women sat in unspoken sorrow, Linnea's eyes started to gleam as she shared her wild idea.

"Guess what I'm going to try to do? You won't believe this one," she said, wanting to surprise Sarah.

"What's the latest idea?" asked Sarah. She knew of her friend's past schemes.

"I'm going to save that house and move it!" Linnea said with a whisper, not wanting anyone to overhear her.

"You're going to *move* the house?" Sarah asked, doubtfully.

Move the whole house? Sarah felt overwhelmed by the idea, even if moving so many times had become a part of the very structure of her cells. But to move more than one's own body and a few personal belongings seemed almost unthinkable to her. To move an entire house was implausible.

"I've looked at it from every angle, and my idea can work. I just know it will work," she said. Linnea was off and running, and she could get that way, much like all the research she poured into her childhood projects.

Move the entire house. Save it and move it. It was simple to Linnea's mind, a woman who knew how to line up tasks and start down the list to check them off. With her logical mind she would approach her big project with the goal of accomplishing all the many steps in order to save and move an old house. But Linnea was not the dreamer, Sarah was, and so when the idea of moving an entire house had come first to Linnea, it was a surprise to Sarah. She tried to imagine a house on wheels, a whole house rolling down tree-lined streets. Although it was a stretch for Sarah, Linnea had a vision firm in her mind of the house moving to its destination, directed by human will, and honored by human determination, with a house mover helping to save it.

"I've been reading articles about the history of house relocation, as it's called, and about house movers. I am learning astounding things," said Linnea.

"I don't know anything about it. I just know it's done occasionally," said Sarah.

"Well, it has happened much more than you would imagine. They have been moving houses in America and Canada for the last few centuries. Across fields, railroad tracks, even over frozen lakes," said Linnea, happy to see most everyone had left the café.

"Frozen lakes?" asked Sarah, in disbelief.

"Yes, I read about one house moving story from a hundred years ago. They pulled an old house by horses across a frozen lake. So many houses have been moved, even on ice, and very few have been lost," she said.

"It doesn't seem safe to move one," said Sarah.

"Good house movers these days guarantee against structural damage. And because old houses are solid and built to last, they move well. Plus almost all house movers know what they are doing," said Linnea.

"That old house on wheels, I don't know. It's hard to imagine, though I like the image," said Sarah, trying again to envision the house on wheels.

"House moving has this incredible history. I've been reading a few books and lots of articles I ordered from libraries all over, even outside our state. I read about Hibbing, Minnesota, where more than a hundred and eighty buildings were moved. It started in the early nineteen-hundreds because they wanted to mine underneath the town."

"You have *got* to be kidding," Sarah stated in disbelief.

"Come down to the newspaper and look it up on the Internet. It's hard to believe what they moved in Hibbing. They moved so many houses, even huge old hotels and store front buildings." Linnea saw Sarah looking as if she did not believe her.

"Why would they want to move so many houses?" asked Sarah.

"There was iron ore underneath the town, so instead of building new houses, people wanted the whole town moved. Some of the houses were offered for free if the workers could pay for them to be moved. I've seen pictures." Linnea said.

"Did you bring any?" ask Sarah.

"Not of those buildings, but I did just find this news article on line about another move. Diane at the newspaper told me about it. It's an old school house, it says 1774," Linnea referred to the article. "It's in New London, Connecticut. It was moved more than once. You won't even believe how many times."

"I can hardly imagine moving a house *once*," said Sarah.

"This school house was moved five times! The last time was in 1988. Maybe in another twenty years they'll move it a sixth time," Linnea joked. "Look at the article, I printed it for you."

Sarah looked at the pictures and read what Linnea gave her. "I see they moved it over and over. Guess they don't know where to keep it. Must be a special old school house to keep saving it," she said.

"The first teacher there was Nathan Hale from the Revolutionary War, that's why they're preserving it," Linnea said. "Can you imagine, *five* times it moved! Tells you how sturdy old buildings can be."

Linnea talked on and on, and the more she spoke, the more Sarah realized her friend had done her research. Sarah then understood why the idea had not come to her first. Linnea was one for setting big goals, and while Sarah was the dreamer, Linnea was the risk taker. As Sarah listened to how it could all possibly work, she became fascinated. She was learning from her old friend just how an entire house moves down the street to fresh ground welcoming its weight and its fate.

Although Sarah had her own feelings to sort out, she was happy for her friend, because at least one of them would get to own a house, and she could certainly visit Linnea and Blair often. Like in childhood, she could partake of the abundance of Linnea's life even if it was never fully Sarah's to claim.

"I've already found a house mover, a man named Everett from Lyle, Illinois," she said, referring to a town about sixty miles to the north.

"You have a house mover already? Why didn't you tell me sooner?" asked Sarah, surprised she had not been included.

"Because I wanted to be certain I could do this. I had to talk to a house mover to learn more, and Everett is the man. He has been moving houses with his dad since he was a boy—he learned from his father. These house movers know what they are doing because it's passed down from generation to generation, like apprenticing in the old days," she said.

Linnea talked on and on about what a good name "Everett" was—what a strong, capable, and unusual name. A good name for a good project, an unusual name for an unusual goal: moving a whole, entire house, saving an old, historic home. Sarah knew Linnea could always sink her teeth into a goal. She believed her friend had the capacity to pull off this big project.

"If anyone can do this, Linnea, you can," Sarah told her.

"You think so? I think I can, but it's a bit intimidating. It's a huge project," Linnea said, sounding somewhat overwhelmed.

"Everyone knows you love a challenge. So, where are you going to put an entire house?" asked Sarah with a smile.

The challenge for a house being offered for moving is almost always where to put it. Many a house had been torn down because there was no good spot to move it to, or the will to find one. More often it was the will. Linnea reminded Sarah that her family had a piece of property down past the road from her parent's stone house, which was on the outskirts of town, near where the water and bluff decided to meet and make a statement of earth.

The land was heavy with trees, and that is when Sarah was startled by where Linnea wanted to move her new, old house.

"Only a pathway of trees would have to be cut," Linnea said, pausing to observe Sarah's face. "Saving this house would save trees I won't need for new construction. Plus the wood from the house won't have to be put in the dump, which is where it all would go if it's torn down."

"But that's our woods! Where we spent half our childhood," Sarah said, stunned.

"I have been researching teardowns and the demolition waste from them, along with waste from new construction. Depending on who you read, it is estimated that it makes up twenty-five to fifty percent of what goes in our dumps! I know I'd have to cut down some trees; it's the price I'd have to pay." She stated this with defiance in her voice as if she were trying to convince not only Sarah but herself.

"I had no idea there is so much waste. I know I've seen more than one dumpster hauled away. Preventing so much going to the dump is another good reason to save the house, besides its history," Sarah added reluctantly.

"To be fair, there is some salvage: metals especially and sometimes wood is kept or occasionally brick. It seems about twenty-five percent—some say higher—is recycled or reused. But still, it's so much waste nationwide," Linnea added.

"Senseless waste. I rather like the charm of an old house and knowing you are helping the environment when you renovate. So when you save and move a house, it's good for nature," Sarah said, knowing she would do anything to be gentle on the earth and to help preserve the earth's trees.

As friends they had always shared a kinship with trees, and so to cut one down seemed to hold in it a hidden crime. They took quite seriously the fate of any tree that might be hacked down. They knew trees once covered much of Illinois and other Midwestern states, but over the last two centuries vast numbers of North American trees had been taken down. Both women thought it odd there was little outcry in the United States about her lost woods or her wounded forests. They understood the earlier centuries of deforestation in America had consequences for current times.

"I've already calculated that the number of trees I'd have to cut down is about one-tenth of the trees it takes to build a new home," Linnea said, while the women stared at one another, both only half-assured because of a forest they each loved. Embedded in their stare was the question of this future act of severing, not only because of their love of trees, but because of the very journey they could only partially understand, with regards to their forest and their close friendship.

Sarah could not imagine cutting down a living tree. She knew she could not do it, even if she understood the human need for building with trees. Sarah was the tree poet. She had spent hours making words work on paper made from trees, capturing her feelings about them: a flowing willow, an ancient poplar, a survivor cottonwood. They were trees she had come to know well while living in Havener since mid-childhood. Sarah had even studied trees of India, and fell in love with an image of one particular tall, elegant tree with rich, orange flower blossoms.

She did not know its pronunciation since her father's language was lost to her. It was an old Sanskrit word, *ashoka*, which she read translated to "without grief." She learned from her reading that the women of India, the land from where half of her ancestry came, ate the flower buds of the *ashoka* tree. She read of the Hindu belief that the water of the flower bud protects children from worry. And she enjoyed knowing Indians believed that a tree will flower only in the places where a woman's foot has stepped. She liked thinking about that idea applying to her own forest where she and Linnea had spent many a happy day.

Trees being one of her passions, she loved when poems about them came to visit her hand. If she did not act in the moment and take pen to paper, her mind and the knowing in her hand would become a blur and then a poem was lost forever. So she had learned to take her sensitive hand as soon as that first line came to her, and with her soft fingers she held a firm pen. She would scratch out a tree poem much like an artist with ink pen would mark on paper the contour of an image, with the soft sounds of a pen filling in the center depth.

Sarah was hesitant when she read her poems to her family. Ty was not a poet by nature and her daughter was only a half-willing listener. But then Julia would work at the kitchen table with her art supplies and draw pictures of trees and hand them to her mother as a casual gift so easily given. And they were good drawings, full of color. They had turquoise limbs and purple leaves, or displayed the glowing autumn radiance of a tree. They made Sarah feel happy about her daughter's growing, and even about her own poems, if indirectly.

Sarah realized she was lost in thought when Linnea broke the silence. "Sarah, I know you love those trees. I promise I'll remove as few as possible. You understand better than most why Blair and I need a home. Besides, I really want to save that historic house," Linnea said emphatically.

"I know you both need a home," Sarah responded with conflicting loyalties to her woods and to her friend in need. "I was just remembering the poem I wrote about the trees." Again the women sat quietly, reflecting on the changes happening.

Linnea had heard Sarah read her tree poems aloud, and they were good poems. Linnea had kept them in a special binder because they were from her friend's tender heart. All this was a reminder of her friend's sensitivity, which made Linnea all the more cautious about the next steps she needed to take because of how they might affect her friend.

Much of the project Linnea had sorted out, except she had not asked the owner of the soon to be torn down house if she could have it—and basically for free. Linnea knew most old houses were given away for free if they were moved. Often just a token dollar was given for a house with a destiny of being saved and moved. Linnea had already discussed the fee for purchasing the house with the house mover, Everett, who told her the only way to take on moving a house is to get it for that token dollar. "Don't pay more than a dollar, or if you have to, a few hundred, at most," Everett advised. He told her houses become available more than one might expect and for free, as hard as it was for her to believe she may become the lucky recipient of one. Linnea had heard of people being given a house for one dollar, but as she discussed further this unusual fact with Sarah, it seemed to both women hard to fathom.

"Did you know houses are given away for a token dollar if they are moved?" asked Linnea.

"I can't imagine someone just giving a house away and for one dollar," Sarah responded, forgetting how imaginative she could be.

"I know; it's hard to believe. But it happens, more than you know. Most houses are offered for a dollar because it saves the owner, or the builder, the cost of tearing it down, and a tear down costs a substantial amount of money," said Linnea.

This remarkable idea, that an entire house could be given away, seemed to both women hard to fathom. For Linnea it was because of not trusting the materialistic values too rampant in her own country or the world for that matter. For Sarah, it was hard enough to imagine having a real home, much less that anyone would want to tear one down or give one away.

5

Links

Sarah knew the couple, Grace and Rolla, who owned the small frame house now at risk of being torn down. She had helped clean up there when illness had hit the family, and they had needed all the help they could get. This was when Sarah had cleaned houses for income; cleaning them was as close as she had come to claiming one as her very own. Dust could touch her fingers, the dust houses collect, but her efforts at cleaning houses had not yet manifested enough money for a home she and her family could call their own.

Linnea remembered Sarah had known the couple, Rolla and Grace Wolter, and she knew she was on good terms with them. Linnea was hesitant to ask Sarah the most awkward of favors. Linnea wanted help in asking the Wolters for the house and for free. She felt uncomfortable making such a huge request to the elderly couple, whom she did not know, and Midwestern ways had taught her it's best to have a link. Linnea also feared the answer to be a "no," and she could not bear to hear such a response directly at this time in her life. She would not hold up well under one more shut door. Too many closed doors in the past two years had left her feeling vulnerable.

Linnea was grieving the loss of her husband, Ray. She had never known such a painful loss, and she was still unsure of how to grieve or even understand what had happened to her small family. Her concern for her daughter's loss was always with her—during Ray's illness and every day since his death. Yet often Linnea would push away her own feelings or memories just to cope with her current life. And her present desire to move a house helped her believe she could go on and create some semblance of a stable life. This also meant she was willing to ask a great deal of her close friend Sarah, when normally she would not make such a request.

Linnea knew she was asking more than she should of her once homeless friend, but she was so determined to save a house and own a home again, she was willing to risk asking Sarah. Linnea was well aware of Sarah's homeless past and how it affected her friend in multiple ways, but after losing Ray she was willing to cross a line she would not have otherwise crossed. She assumed it would not risk their friendship. Nothing could ever do that, in either woman's heart. They had spoken of this more than once, how their friendship would survive no matter what. Neither one could ever imagine anything that would come between them. Their friendship felt that sure, that bed-rocked.

But Linnea was sensitive to her friend's position in life with no family left except the one she was creating and her strong ties with Linnea's family. For Sarah, Tyler, and Julia there was no home to call their own, no title in hand that showed ownership, no claim to private property. All they had was a small rented apartment that had been made to feel like a home. It was a temporary haven.

It had been a week since Linnea had first spoken with Sarah in person about the potential house move, so she stopped by the café where she worked. Both women were sitting once again at a table in a back corner, chatting, when Linnea finally stated what she wanted to say.

"I wish I didn't have to ask this, I regret having to ask you. But, Sarah, you know the Wolters. I know this is a huge favor, but would you ask them if I can have the house...for a dollar?"

When Linnea made her imposition on her friend with a homeless past, Sarah had by that time thought so much about the plan, and understanding Linnea's needs, she felt willing to help. Sarah knew how much Linnea needed this because of her husband's unexpected death. She understood how her friend was still grieving and at a loss of how to get a house again. Even though Sarah had a longing for a home, she put her own desires aside, which was what she often did. Sarah had learned how to transcend her own self, partly because she'd had a mother who was mentally ill, and partly because in her own soul she knew when something was the right thing to do. She could then easily give of herself, no matter how transcendent it meant she needed to be.

Sarah recalled nursing her mother during a bout of physical and mental illness wrapped together like some twisted, distorted vine. It was both difficult and simple to give at those moments. Difficult because then one's own life purpose had to be put on hold. Simple because that is what life demands and in the end gives meaning and direction to one's purpose. So Sarah wrapped up like a treasured gift her feelings about her deepest desire to have a house and home. Sacrificing her own desire for a stable home was simple when her altruism took hold, even if it left an unfulfilled desire inside her. Sarah knew as she listened to Linnea's request that she would tell her yes. She felt determined to help her friend.

"Linnea, of course I will help you. I'd be glad to ask

Grace Wolter," said Sarah warmly.

"You will? Despite the trees you love?" Linnea said, relieved.

"I've thought about all the issues regarding the trees and your solution seems to be a compromise. Yes, I will help you. You're my friend, and you and your family have given me so much," Sarah shared. "I recall hearing Grace Wolter talk about the hardship for people escaping slavery and how her family tried to help. I would also like to see that Underground Railroad house saved."

"You would?" Linnea responded.

"Yes. I have been reading up on the Underground Railroad and what people — black and white — sacrificed for freedom. It's a fascinating if a painful history. You know, not everyone knows about the Underground Railroad, even in America, much less other parts of the world," she said.

"You're right. It's not as well known as it should be," Linnea confirmed. "I wish I knew more."

"We'll learn more, and maybe we can help others to know about it," Sarah said optimistically.

"You are unbelievable. You're such a wonderful friend," Linnea said as she got up from her chair and hugged her. Sarah hugged her back but Linnea was surprised when she felt an unfamiliar distance from Sarah.

Linnea teased that they could all live together again, in her potential house: Linnea and her daughter Blair, with Sarah, Julia, and Tyler. Sarah wished it could work, but both knew it was too much of a long shot now that they were adults. Besides, Sarah could not give up her hope to one day own a home for her small family, without needing Linnea's help.

Linnea also knew she was not ready to share a home. It had been a long two years since her husband's illness, and his death had filled her with a sorrow she could neither understand nor defy. Sarah understood such pain, having lost both her parents early, and knew her friend deserved better than she had received. Linnea had been good to Ray as he died too drawn out a death, like an autumn leaf slowly fading, leaving, but far too soon. So many seasons Linnea and Ray would not see together, and the fall that had been their last left such sadness, if also a fulfillment of her being there for Ray. It was an odd sense of fulfillment, one that can only be known from loving and caring for a dying person, even if mixed with deep grief.

Sarah knew Linnea needed this project to help her cope with the loss of Ray, and she needed a house for Blair and for their future. For so long Sarah had not seen her friend this animated about anything. Although Linnea's family had some means, they were not wealthy. Most small-town, family-owned newspapers were as much a labor of love and community, as a business. So this project, even if risky, sounded like the chance Linnea needed to move on with her life, starting over on her own as the only living parent for Blair. Besides, Linnea had lost her first home, one she and Ray had purchased before he became ill, as the small equity they had built was taken by medical bills. Sarah told herself the losses that family had endured were greater than her own. Still, a part of her knew her own losses were paramount in her life, as she well understood a person does not recover quickly from childhood homelessness and its multiple sorrows.

With her own sadness put aside, Sarah told Linnea she would ask the Wolters on the upcoming weekend. She was sorry to know they were selling their house but had heard they were leaving the town of their birth for a warmer climate, as illness altered their course. People were relieved when Rolla Wolters had rallied from his illness, but many would be sad to see them leave town.

Circumventing her own feelings and needs, Sarah was concerned about not hurting the owner's feelings about the house. But as she and Linnea talked, it occurred to them that Rolla and Grace might be glad someone cared enough to save their home.

Sarah recalled looking at old family photos in their hallway while hearing stories from Mrs. Wolter about the house, as Grace liked to talk of her family's past. Grace Wolter still had pride about their home being part of the many links in Illinois to the Underground Railroad. She knew it could not equal the courage it took for people young and old escaping slavery, but she thought her family had helped in some small way to support people who were "freedom seekers." Grace told Sarah that was a more accurate term, freedom seekers, than fugitive slaves, and it was the truth spoken.

Grace showed Sarah a map in a book she had been sent from a woman author, completed after thirty years of research — a true labor of love — that traced all the Underground Railroad lines in Illinois. They were like vertical waves throughout the state and Sarah thought they looked like streams of goodwill flowing in patterns south to north, an ethereal railroad much like her unearthly fantasy house from childhood. But as elusive as the Underground Railroad was, it indeed was an actual, insistent course on the road to freedom. No, it was not an actual railroad, as her daughter Julia had asked when imagining a secret railroad under the earth. It was, however, a very real route, with stops in the homes of people willing to act upon their beliefs and help people escape slavery.

Grace Wolter's great-great-grandparents felt strongly about their anti-slavery views. She explained how people from different faiths helped, such as the Quakers, Congregationalists, and Presbyterians. Her relatives were Quakers committed to human dignity and willing to give a hand to anyone looking for freedom, even at their own risk, even if it meant hiding people in their home. The house, built by Grace's great-great-grandfather, had been passed down from generation to generation. All three women knew the house held an important role in their town's past and even in American history. It was a unique time when people of both racial backgrounds joined forces to work together for a just cause. Sarah hoped she would learn more from Grace to better understand the past, and then planned to share it with Linnea and their daughters. She thought the house with its wise heritage could be one of the best history lessons Julia and Blair could have about U.S. history.

Sarah had been a good listener to Grace because it made Sarah feel she belonged to the past, to the human story. She felt at peace while hearing an elder's personal heritage. At times it was an odd serenity, that which comes from the perspective of history, even with all of history's failings. But somehow Sarah belonged to it; she could even identify with freedom seekers even though she did not understand why. Other times, when Sarah heard the voice of an elder friend, she felt the words were poetry, currents in a stream of life, and that brought her a contented peace. Sarah loved those precious oral histories and the emotions they arose in her.

As she had looked deeply into the sepia-toned photos that lined the hallways of the old house, she could almost imagine she had some heritage or family root that she could cautiously build upon. She had been stripped of that knowledge of kin, of greats and great greats, so she was left with a hole she did not quite grasp. But when she intently studied the soft brown photos on the wall, she felt a fractured bit of her own history start a sort of mending. Such was her ability to re-create family ties for herself, or at least to heal.

Sarah did have one fervent memory of her own, of

her father taking her on his lap and in his husky voice singing to her, "Chittigong, Chittigong, that is your song." He then told Sarah the story of her great-great grandfather, an Ayurvedic doctor with herbs, who had lived in a town called Chittigong. And then he would sing his chant again as if he were in some far off vision of his own making. "Chittigong, Chittigong, that is your song."

That memory had once given her the impulse to visit the local junior college and study various maps of India. She found Chittigong in what is now Bangladesh, which before 1971 had been East Pakistan, and before that the Bengal region of India. Chittigong was a small city near Burma, now called Myanmar. It was on the other side of the earth from Sarah's current home, yet in some way she knew it was the center of the world for her paternal family memory.

Much like her early life, her memory of a distant familial place still felt elusive to Sarah. What was real to her now were links to people in a small Illinois town, a place where she felt some sense of belonging, though not fully rooted. And Mrs. Wolter was one of her guides in her small town life, helping her to feel more a part of the world. Sarah was grateful for knowing this caring woman. It was then Sarah knew Grace Wolter would be the person to sit with, drink sweetened tea, and to broach the subject of buying the old house for one dollar.

For some reason both Sarah and Linnea stayed anxious about this planned discussion. They did not realize they would save the Wolter family lots of money, as the agreement for the property sale had been for Grace and Rolla Wolter to pay for half the demolition fee of the house, which would cost nearly ten thousand dollars total. The couple had been so concerned they might lose the builder's interest they offered to pay half, accommodating more than they should or even needed.

Sarah's offer would be welcomed words on all accounts. Someone had mentioned to Mr. and Mrs. Wolter that they could offer up the house to be moved. But they thought no one would be interested in their humble house. They knew it was worthy because Grace's great-great-grandparent's sweat helped to create and build their home as a refuge for their family and many people on the Underground Railroad.

Rolla Wolter had said to his wife more than once, "It would be a shame for this house to go all in a rubble. People worked hard to build this house. It took real sweat to make such a place back then, even today it takes hard labor to build. Then, there's my sweat to just to keep her going." He would hang his head, shaking it with resigned remorse, saying as if in preliminary grief, "This house has such a history."

6

An Invisible River

Sarah set up the meeting with Mrs. Wolter for that coming Saturday morning. Tyler could take Julia to a park or out bike riding since good weather looked promising. Sarah wanted to do her meeting alone, as she had yet to tell her husband what she and Linnea were planning. She didn't know why she felt she had to keep it private but sensed it was not a good time to discuss it with him. Ty had a certain streak that worried Sarah at times; he was more defiant than she. Somehow she figured the house idea might seem inequitable to him, that Linnea could get the house and for nothing.

Sarah knew how protective he was of her, of her hurts and wounds, and how frustrated he was that he had not provided her with a house. She knew that as a man he had some deep longing for the ability to provide. It was not to be a man of the house but more that he had all the skills to build a home but not the outlet for those talents. Both thought they would have faired better in colonial times when the house you knew was the one you raised up with your own hands and hard work. Neighbors helped one another back then because it was their way, or they had to for survival. Or maybe she and Tyler would have been happier in a tribe, Sarah thought, native born to the soil and roaming to the gulf coast in winter and in summer, moving further north for the cool, being attuned to nature's rhythms. Sarah longed for such a freedom connected to nature.

Sarah knew Tyler and she had a need at times to get in their old blue truck and drive on long country roads past farms stretched out on the horizon. She linked this need to American Indian roots held in the land, as if an invisible heritage still remained living there. It was as if a knowing in the land itself, from a past century when the Potawatomi Indians rode with Chief Aptakisic had left hidden wisdom for Sarah in the twenty-first century. She assumed past native tribes were freer than she could ever be. She thought her and Tyler's roaming urge must go back to some very early need to feel true freedom, which she understood could only be carried out within nature.

Such early instincts, be they for freedom or roaming, had been left to smolder not just in her Tyler, but in many men Sarah saw in the café where she worked late breakfasts and lunches. She could even identify with their frustration, but she did not take it to bitterness. The world to her had more sweetness than harm. It was not worth the inner sacrifice to take pain and make bricks of resentment. She would rather feel her raw pain as that was load enough.

Still, the men she observed at her café job caused her to feel empathy for their loneliness. She wished she could do something to change it, wished she had some way to relieve their pain, but for now all she could do was keep focused on her own family's survival and help her closest friend, Linnea. She thought maybe she would gain some insight about what she could do to help some people, while riding with Tyler on one of her cherished country rides, past creeks with quivering tree limbs and farms with the promise of knee-high corn in summer.

"Sarah, let's go out for a drive," Tyler would say, feeling restless.

"I'm ready," she'd tell him.

"I'm itching to be on that country road," he'd say, and so was she.

She loved those drives. After a time of riding, with Tyler at the wheel, she would slip into an altered realm where she sensed an undercurrent, as if it ran through her and the land, like an invisible river. Then she would intuit American Indian tribes, people who once knew the very breath of the land, as if they whispered their truths to her. One had to listen carefully but the sounds were there, in the wind, in one's inner knowing. Then the wind of time would move, as if a veil was flowing from one century into the next, back and forth between history and its sorrows and concurrent truths. Sarah could feel this history, of a people who walked before her, as if their shadow was gently upon her own humble life, fulfilling some hidden desire, encouraging some unseen truth.

It was a history of a people from both North America and from her father's land of birth. Even if Sarah had never traveled out of the country, she had "visited" the Indian subcontinent through her reading and research. Thus the ancients with whom she felt she could merge, with timelessness as her aid, were not only American Indians, but East Indians. Sarah sensed a whole other reality intuitively when she traveled country roads, sensing another era of centuries and cultures before her—not so long ago in the true scope of time—calling to her. The land of America called to Sarah like a constant beating drum, a sound as old as the hills. The ancient culture of India reached to her and sang of its woes and its multiple wisdoms from thousands of years past.

Then it was as if time lost its perimeter, and Sarah became part of a vortex of energy filtering into the world.

It was brought into her elastic thinking but even more into her subtle feelings, her intuitive knowing. Sarah was bridging cultures and centuries, linking past and present in a global viewpoint of unity, with multiple truths becoming a whispered knowingness inside her depths, even if she was just beginning to understand this linkage and inner knowing.

Those intuitions were left by an ancient people who walked before her quietly in a forest, with soft crackling of small tree branches in America, or the pattering of bare feet on hardened, smooth mud paths in India. Such good, from tribes or cultures past, she could discern through her extra abilities, sensing its force, its reality, transcendent of time, finding its way into her heart. Like a poem come to rest.

"What're you thinking about? You've been quiet," Tyler asked.

"Just thinking," she said softly, so he left her alone with her thoughts. Tyler drove in silence to keep his frustrations at bay and accepted their sparse conversation.

Sarah and Tyler had enjoyed taking drives in their truck ever since they had been together. Lately Sarah had needed those rides all the more because so much was happening in her life with Linnea and within her own self. So with Tyler driving and Sarah quiet on those country roads, she began discovering a sense of her place in the world of sunlight or a hint of her power under a night sky of stars. She felt as if she was made of the same stardust in an expanse of sparkling stars, and of the same walk of peoples east and west, native or brown, black or white. In this knowing, in this gentle awareness of unity, Sarah was quietly finding her own inner power.

She aligned with a larger realm, in part because of her own family story, and in part because she could transcend the past. It was in this reality of connectedness, of her personal heritage and with all people from a world's history, and of varied racial identities, she felt as Sarah could feel—a oneness with the human race. This alignment, this complete connectedness, was just one of the wisdoms whispered by her inner voice while moving on dusty roads.

She was also discovering another hidden truth. She was finding her own sense of empowerment as a woman. Like many women around the globe, Sarah was coming into her own, from her reality of truth, from her sense of power. It was the power of love, not the love of power over others. It was a power to just be, without any need to do or to prove oneself. It was the power linked to nature and to tender connectedness between people. It was the power of complete self-acceptance without any need for external approval. It was the power of unconditional acceptance. It was the core of love.

Sarah was discovering her inner world, her inner core, as they drove on farm roads with the dust of stone, a shimmering silica left behind in their absence. Sarah and Tyler roamed like the Indian people before them, their old truck as their freedom ride, while she drew from the silky blue sky an inner strength, which slowly was expanding her sense of her self and her strength. On those country roads past native cornfields, Sarah, in harmony with herself, aligned with her sense of God, who still remained as flexible as the wind and forever compassionate.

Sarah also realized it was the 1853 house and its potential move that kept leading her down her new path of awareness. It was as if the wisdom held in the walls of that simple house started guiding her. It was an intangible but solid force, one that had led the way for past freedom seekers on the Underground Railroad. Now it was a light shown for her in some mysterious way she could not yet put into words. But the illumination was there all the same. It was a house full of light guiding her to a more unified place. It was as if the same brilliance in the light of the lanterns, hung on the designated side of a house to let freedom seekers know it was safe to approach the house on the Underground Railroad, was still alive two centuries later and lighting the pathway for Sarah. This time it was a light inside her own soul illuminating her inner journey.

On her most recent truck ride with Tyler, Sarah rode in the silence of her awareness. During their last few drives in the expanse of gently rolling farms, all her concerns were put in perspective. She had made peace with the fact that the 1853 house Linnea desperately hoped to move would not be Sarah's home. She was prepared for Tyler's potential reactions, as she had yet to tell him, but that now concerned her less. Most importantly, her own fears about never having a home of her own were quieted. She trusted she'd be shown a way to her own place, to a house she would call home.

All details of the complications of her life at the beginning of the millennium drifted easily out of her mind as she tapped her inner world and stretched her essence on the plains. She had the whole picture put together in her mind, so now she had solace in her heart. Now she could proceed with Mrs. Wolter. Now she felt her own sense of power in her planned act of asking. Knowing that power was all Sarah wanted.

7

Answers to Prayers

Saturday morning Sarah found herself sitting at the wooden table chitchatting with Grace Wolter. She loved the feel of Grace's kitchen, always had liked it when she worked there cleaning with a calm presence she brought to the task. The room was a respite from the harsh realities life could bring. Once an old boyfriend who knew of the burden of her homeless past told Sarah, "It's your cross to bear." But she questioned his statement. She perceived there were many crosses not worthy to bear and others were manmade and not made for heavenly reasons.

She rather wanted to live with the hope she had once read on a small, green and silver plaque in an antique shop: "Earth Has No Sorrow That Heaven Cannot Heal." And for a homeless child, who had lost both her parents, to grow into a woman with this understanding, well, anyone who knew of this hope also knew of Sarah's integrity. Not many knew, only a few did, and Grace Wolter was one of them.

"It is good to see you again, Sarah. It's been too long since we sat and had hot tea together," Grace said warmly.

"It has been too long," Sarah said. "I've been busy with a new project. It has been a bit hectic." Sarah paused, and then added, "You know, Linnea is without a house now; she is at her parents' home temporarily."

"Yes, dear, I heard about Ray's death. I'm sorry for her and her family. He was so ill and so young a man. And then to lose the house, it's a shame," said Grace with sympathy.

"It was sad, Mrs. Wolter. Linnea has been through a difficult time." Sarah hesitated before she asked. "You know, Linnea has this unusual idea. I think you know how she can be."

"Oh, we all surely do. She can be one determined woman," said Mrs. Wolter knowingly.

"Well, she heard your house is going to be torn down, and she thinks she can save it. She even wants to move it, believe it or not," Sarah said hesitantly.

"You mean she would want this house? And do you mean to tell me she can get it moved?" Grace asked, clearly stunned.

"Linnea seems to think she can, and I do, too. She talked to a house mover. She has a pretty complicated plan worked out, and I'll be helping her." Sarah paused for a moment, gauging Mrs. Wolter's reaction. Sarah then told her about Linnea's strategy, telling her all about their efforts together. Mrs. Wolter listened intently and then had a broad smile and clapped her hands.

"Once again, Sarah, you are an answer to a prayer. First you answered my prayers with polish and goodwill, when you helped during Rolla's illness. But this time, you are goodwill magnified!"

And when she said magnified, her eyes lit up like the eyes of some of the homeless people Sarah had seen as a child, and as she had seen in her own mother's eyes at times. The difference was this joy was grounded and not the sometimes startled-eye look Sarah had witnessed too often, too early. She recalled those lost looks that reflected either the sorrow of mental illness or the result of the multiple losses of the homeless persons Sarah had observed compassionately.

"It will save us a good deal of money," Grace said with relief. "And I am very glad to know this house, with such a rich history, will live on."

Sarah had not expected such an elated response from Grace. But when Sarah heard how much money it would save the hard-working couple who were about to enter what few golden years were left, she smiled as well. It would cost ten thousand dollars or more to pay for the teardown plus dumping fees at the landfill, but now their half, a full five thousand dollars would be a savings. And one more unique house would be saved from demolition and from being put in the dump.

"I have to tell you, Sarah. The builders, Joel and Chuck, told me they don't really want to tear it down because of its history. They didn't know about the Underground Railroad connection until after they bought it. We should have told them but with Rolla sick, we just had to sell in a hurry. I think they'll be glad you are going to move it and I expect will work with you. Plus, it will save their share of the cost of the tear down," Grace said happily.

"Then it's a win-win, isn't it?" Sarah pointed out with a smile, and Grace smiled back.

Sarah looked around the kitchen with its birch wood cabinets and honey-colored wood floor of narrow maple. She imagined sitting one day at Linnea's kitchen table in the home, watching Julia and Blair. Sarah could envision them in her mind's eye, drawing with intense colors and then laughing, much like she and Linnea had when they were young and almost as carefree as their daughters seemed.

Sarah loved thinking about her Julia. She was proud of the daughter she was rearing and of the parenting she was providing. She understood how to nurture her child's creative spirit and as a result Julia was curious, industrious, and always making things. "A busy child is a happy child," Sarah's mother used to say, words passed down and still in Sarah's memory. It was one of the few hints Sarah had of some link to a family heritage on her mother's side. Sarah refined the saying in different ways, stating, "A creative child is a happy child." As Sarah knew, most if not all children were creative in one way or another, if it was not squeezed out of them by hearing "no" too often or having too many societal expectations.

On other occasions Sarah would think to herself, "A contemplative child is a happy child." Sarah saw in Julia not just the ability to create, but also a welcomed, reflective nature. Especially at bedtime, when her daughter was settled down for the night, with lights dim, Julia would share her inner world. Those were some of the best moments every mother or father learns to cherish, of soft words shared and then a sheet tucked in over the shoulder, with cheeks of tender skin gently kissed, and a child smiling with contentment. Sarah appreciated the ritual each night; because even if she did not have a house she owned, she had a place she had made a home. And having been homeless herself, she never took it for granted.

Yes, Sarah could imagine visiting Linnea with Julia in that very house where she sat with Grace, a house built nearly a hundred and fifty years ago, and that had "raised" four generations of family already and now would have the chance to raise a fifth with Linnea and Blair. The kitchen light filtering in the windows warmed her thoughts, just as seeing Grace's smile filled her heart.

She watched the older woman as she rustled through papers regarding the house, with Sarah admiring her energy and the way her gray hair was swept up on top of her head. Sarah wondered how long it was, what other color it had been, and how Grace had decided to keep her hair long when so many older women cut theirs short. Sarah pondered what her own hair would be like when she was seventy-five years old and what would motivate her to have the drive she saw in Grace Wolters. Would Sarah's skin also have that lovely translucence aging can bring? She reflected on how it would feel for both Mr. and Mrs. Wolter to leave their home. As her mind processed her curious thoughts, Sarah suddenly heard Mrs. Wolter speaking to her.

"Here is the finalized paper, Sarah. I've signed it. It says Linnea can have the house after we move out of our home in about three or four weeks. We can go and get it notarized if you like, if you think it's best," suggested Grace.

"I don't think it's necessary. We know each other and that will be good enough for Linnea. We're a small town. A person's word is still good," Sarah responded.

As Grace Wolter handed over the signed paper, Sarah felt awed and humbled. She heard Grace say in her quiet breath of a voice, made softer by years gone by, "Oh, I will miss this home. It's hard to leave it behind, you know. It has such memories for our family. It's been a good home to us, and to my parents, and our relatives before them."

Sarah knew Grace's husband, Rolla, had health concerns that were paramount, so the good couple had to leave for a different climate. She was sorry to see them go, even if Sarah felt joy in knowing that Linnea and Blair could have the home. It helped when Grace told her of the added benefits of giving the home away.

"It makes it easier to let it go, knowing Linnea and Blair will find our house useful. And you, too, Sarah. I hope you can enjoy it as well, and keep its history alive. You know, we have a diary from my relative begun in the eighteen fifties, with some references about its Underground Railroad history. I'll try to leave a copy for you and Linnea before we go. It's been quite a while since I have read it," Grace told her.

"I look forward to reading it," Sarah said with excitement, when hearing of the rare documentation of the Underground Railroad. "I haven't heard you talk about the diary."

"We have kept that in the family, until now. We're lucky to have something in writing about the courageous people they helped. It wasn't safe back then to keep records about the Underground Railroad. It was a well kept secret in my great-great-grandmother's diary. It's something to read what she dared to write," said Grace, her eyes sparkling with memory.

"I promise I'll do my best to keep the story going. Julia and Blair will be very interested in the Underground Railroad. I think it will be good for me to be part of passing down the history. You have told me many wonderful stories about the past," said Sarah, thinking of her own father's stories.

Grace Wolter had also heard some of Sarah's stories of her past. She knew of Sarah's childhood homelessness, though many did not. Grace wanted to ask why Linnea was taking their nearly ancient house and not Sarah, but like many Midwesterners she thought it may be too personal a question. Instead she hinted, asking indirectly.

"So, Linnea is the one to take the house. That's interesting. I am glad it will not be torn down."

"Linnea is the one who needs it more," Sarah answered directly. She preferred to be more straightforward, as her mother had been. "Besides, Linnea had the idea. I don't think I would have come up with it. She has been through a hard time with Ray's death." And in Sarah's way of giving, she added, "I'm glad the opportunity came to Linnea. And it's been a good experience helping her with the house moving idea."

Mrs. Wolter recognized altruism when she saw it, had known it in her own family heritage when they risked their security because they were against slavery, and she had seen it with Linnea's parents when they took Sarah in. Now she watched the beauty of it wash over Sarah's soft-toned face.

Sarah, on the other hand, was aware of both her desire to give and her desire to receive. In her past, those wishes would have been more at odds, but after her country drives and new way of seeing her world, she was content with both. Still, she so wanted a home but she did not speak of the longing inside her. She kept that desire private, finding it difficult to put into words what she was discovering within herself on her country drives and where she hoped it would lead her.

Although Sarah could start to imagine a home for her and her family, she still could not fathom a house being bought for one dollar, even if it would cost plenty to move it and put it on a new foundation. In all her years of wandering as a homeless child, she never would have imagined herself in that house, at that kitchen table, pulling out a crisp new dollar bill, which Linnea and she had ceremoniously picked for this very occasion. And as Sarah, the deliverer of that unusual dollar bill, handed it to Grace, both women young and old, linked eyes while time halted and history changed. Both assumed it would be for the better and Sarah knew, in her quiet chamber, which claimed all truth, it would be for the best. This old house could never let anyone down; it was just that solid.

It had never let down any freedom seekers. It had been a haven years ago when blacks and whites risked everything for the sake of their commitment to freedom. It had been a critical haven for many a family a century and a half ago, a respite stop, when at other times there was no safe house. Often a woods or riverfront was the only hiding place, which made the run toward freedom all the more remarkable. No symbolic house could ever equal the risk taken or the courage of people who ran hard for their freedom. Still, the fact that many opened their homes to assist others in their search for freedom, and that Grace's house was such a home, gave Sarah a sense of respect. The goodwill and dignity stored in a house now being gifted for a dollar was a house destined to continue its calling as a haven on the road to a better life in the twenty-first century.

Sarah had wanted to ask to look around the house but felt it was an intrusive request given the couple had to filter out the stuff of their lives and then let go. She had cleaned only half the rooms of the house, staying downstairs when she had worked for them, so she knew the house only half well. The parlor was on the left side and the dining room on the right as one entered the front door, duplicating many houses Sarah and Linnea had visited in their home town over the years.

Sarah had cleaned and polished in the parlor and dining room, buffing mirrored reflections in the end tables and on an old china cabinet. She sprayed and wiped the glass over old photos hugging walls as they claimed a personal and private history for one family. She had arranged dining room chairs just so, and polished the dark, shiny dining table under the ceiling light until it left a glow, like soft fog.

Mostly though, she focused on the kitchen, giving it the kind of good clean that brought women the satisfaction of a job well done. It was that simple fulfillment of a good scrub. Sarah had at the time wondered about different women all over the world and how they felt when their kitchens were clean. She thought about stoves and counters, or simple homes with earthen floor and fire for cooking, and how those women felt when they too put all in tidy order, like the completion of a chapter in a book when the reader closes the pages and begins another attempt at living in the world.

Sarah had liked working in the home Rolla and Grace kept. Now she was the recipient of a paper that said the same house would be given as a gift. Sarah held the paper from Mrs. Wolter close, as if its fusion with her body would enable her to find the key to her own house. As she stood up reluctantly, Sarah and Grace began their sweet goodbyes, as they knew this would be one of their last times together, one of their last hugs. This woman, who felt more like an adopted grandmother than a former employer, would not remain in Sarah's life as she knew it.

Sadly, she said, "I have to go now; Linnea is waiting for me. I need to let her know what you decided."

"Yes, I know dear; I know you have to go," said Grace, adding, "I will miss your sweet face. Let me walk you out. I do hope you will write to us; we love to get mail. Maybe Linnea can send us a copy, now and then, of the local newspaper."

"I'm sure Linnea would be more than happy to send you the local newspaper every week!" said Sarah with a smile, thinking of the house Grace Wolter had just given to Linnea and Blair.

They stepped on to the front porch, which had been glassed in for protection from the winter weather, something many people had once done to their old-fashioned porches. This rather odd addition offset the front of the house, hiding its smack-dab-in-the-middle front door. The walk to the door, and on to the porch and then outside, down the steps, was a ritual familiar to Sarah in her small town. People always walked a special visitor outside, as it helped to ease the reluctance of farewells.

As the women said their final goodbyes, Sarah was sadness and happiness braided together in a rhythm that felt like a coursing river pushing her life forward on its own accord. She had known the same remarkable feeling when she first stood near the cliff at Linnea's childhood home, when wind was not just a singular power but a force far greater than any she could devise. It was the wind of the future. It was the wind of a destiny she could not clearly see, but sensed every time such force and wind occurred. And this time it felt as if the wind would nearly carry her away.

8

Truths

Sarah felt joy in her bones as she walked to where Linnea waited. It was a good thing to be the bearer of happy news, and both women needed this: Sarah as a carrier and Linnea as the recipient. Because even though Linnea looked like the rational and strong woman, and Sarah the more vulnerable and sensitive, the reverse was true at this time in their female stories. Linnea did not realize what Sarah knew well — that her ability to be vulnerable was a strength — even if this understanding went against the culture at large. But when cities spit you out homeless on curbs, lessons are learned, and Sarah took them in as a poet would, with a sensitive eye.

Linnea needed this good news almost as much as she needed to weep at her husband's gravesite, though she could not. Her house moving idea had occupied her thinking in a manner of denial as much as hope. All the energy of the last two years with him ill, which she felt had been poured away, was currently filtering like a clean stream into her house moving plan. She knew if her husband were alive he would have smiled at her research about house moving and would have been amused and impressed. Yet with him alive she would never have needed to make this drastic leap. She wondered if she was losing her mind to even consider moving an old house.

But Sarah had told her clearly, "I have been around enough people losing it to know the signs. I will be the first to tell you if you cross that line, Linnea." That was a comfort to Linnea in the uncharted waters of grief, which she did not understand. Linnea had watched Sarah when she grieved, tears flowing without a hint of her trying to repress them. That image helped Linnea, but there was still much territory which the river of her pain needed to pass before her grief and heart would better heal.

Linnea could see Sarah walking toward her. Sarah's movement in the distance had a pulse like her own heartbeat. Linnea felt her world was changing, swept up into courage and pain. As she watched her friend walk she tried to see if Sarah's movement gave her the answer of the new beginning for which her heart longed. Life had felt so unsettled since Ray died and their home was gone. Just keeping their first house would have meant she could hold on to those memories of him, of times they had laughed or argued in their living room, or of the bedroom where their child had been conceived, or the small room carefully prepared for their baby.

Bringing home Blair when she was a newborn gave Linnea the most tenuous feeling she had ever allowed herself. That vulnerability was not familiar to her mind, which lined up all the details of life. Ray's death, even if she stood by him faithfully, made her want to hide again from her sense of vulnerability. His death was the greatest sorrow Linnea had ever known, and she just wished she had a neat little room where she could let down and feel all that was meant to be felt when a woman is filled with grief.

Linnea remembered a time when she saw Sarah's raw grief, when news came that her mother had died, alone, cold, and homeless. She saw Sarah's very large tears like round spheres, far more similar to dewdrops, softly falling on Sarah's cheeks. Her teardrops seemed to almost defy the pull of gravity while Sarah was grief magnified.

Sarah's quiet grief had begun to free Linnea in some way she was just now starting to understand. It was as if when Sarah grieved, she grieved not only for herself in her private pain, but for the world as a whole, for the earth in all its sorrow, for the homeless in all theirs. It was as if the whole world was set upside down, a globe turned on its axis, and pain knew no boundaries of country or culture. Sarah was a grief carrier of the world, and her round tears lessened some of the grief of the earth's sorrowful, half-shattered people.

But today, on this April morning when the sun shown through the cold spring air like crisp sparks that awakened Linnea to her inner world, Sarah was not the carrier of grief, but of promise. Linnea could tell even before they spoke because as Sarah came closer, her walking bones had a bounce to them that spoke of more than the beauty of the day. It was the walk of good news. Linnea could hardly believe her good fortune.

When Sarah approached, she pulled out both pockets of her jeans, showing her friend they were empty. The dollar bill was gone, put into the hands of Grace. The playful gesture was one from childhood, as if both could regress now to younger years where skipping was the order of the day.

Sarah smiled. "I bought the house! For one dollar! I just love being this kind of banker," she told her joyously.

"You bought me a house, Sarah? You didn't! For one dollar? It's unbelievable," said Linnea, stunned by her friend's words.

Now Linnea could hardly contain herself. She held

on to Sarah and circled round with her, for joy was no stranger to either. Joy helped carry them through their childhood and once again it renewed their bond of friendship. Sarah went on to tell Linnea about all the details, of the beautiful kitchen wood floor, Grace's swept up gray hair, and the way in which Linnea's offer would help that gentle couple. Both were ecstatic and all the specifics that kept streaming forth just enlarged their scope of anticipation.

"This is an amazing day," Sarah announced. "You have a house for a dollar and the chance to move it."

"I have to sit down. It's hard to take it all in, Sarah. You did it!" Linnea exclaimed.

"Guess what else. Mrs. Wolter has a diary her great, great Grandmother kept during the years they were part of the Underground Railroad. She said she will make a copy for us to keep and share with others," Sarah said intensely. "Here is the letter saying the house is yours."

Sarah showed her the letter, words put in writing, solid words on tangible paper, telling Linnea she could have the house within a month's time, as long as she could raise it and then move it within the next two months before they expected to move south. Moving it seemed the smaller of the two tasks. Getting the house was the huge bridge Linnea had doubted could be crossed and she well understood how Sarah helped her to cross it, at no small price emotionally. Linnea knew how much Sarah wanted to own a house. She could have desired the dollar house for herself and her family, but instead Sarah was selfless and helped Linnea to acquire the house.

Such is love between true friends, Linnea thought, love that rises up like the wind, without conditions. It was much like the wind of the bluffs around the teal blue lake, wind that came suddenly for no cause except to show its beauty and strength. It was a powerful love these women shared, unconditionally; a love that knew infinity could become a worldly reality.

As children they would tease and compete with grand statements, "I love you as much as all the millions of stars in the universe," moving to, "I love you more than the billions of stars in the universe." It was Sarah's statement that left them breathless: "I love you infinity times infinity." Their child bodies stood very still as their minds worked at grasping a concept not many adults would even conceive, much less try to experience as expansive love. This house gifting day was one of those moments of love, when infinity became an earthly reality. Sarah had given a gift of the heart and Linnea would know gratitude multiplied.

As for Sarah, she grasped her power more fully. She did not realize she could feel this empowered until now. Somehow a house of her own seemed closer at hand because she had given one away. Not that it was really hers to give away, but for that brief day she knew a house had passed between her hands, her soft fingers being a link once again to a bit more healed of a world. And this new sense inside Sarah, of her own power, kept her hoping it would ultimately lead her to a house she could make a home, not only in her imagination, but in the tangible, earthly world.

9

Doors

Tyler had been secretly working on the imaginary door, or rather the real door first created in Sarah's imagination. He thought at least he could start on the door of their dream house, and it gave him a hope and an outlet for the angst that steeped inside him. He worked on it through his lunch time at the small company where he was employed to design and cut fretwork — or house gingerbread that had decorated many porches and roof lines of old houses for well over a century. The trim was shipped all over the country, sometimes even overseas from the factory where Tyler had worked hard for the last ten years. Because his woodworking was so highly respected, he was given privileges, like being able to work on his own wood over his lunch hour.

The door would be his surprise for Sarah, a Christmas gift he needed to start on early since time was scarce for him to cherish the feel of wood — his wood — under his fingers. It had to be oak, which had cost him a pretty penny, and it had to be a Dutch door, which cut in half, made it easier to work on and had reduced the cost of the wood. He remembered the day he bought the oak from the lumber shop down by the train tracks. The salesman looked at him without saying a word. Tyler didn't know if the man was thinking he was half-crazy for working on such a fancy door without having any house to put it on. Then he caught himself, realizing this man did not know him or his situation, as Tyler was more isolated from people. Tyler was not like most folks in town who were linked in some way and knew one other. It was usually a link of goodwill though Havener was not without its problem citizens.

Tyler's intent, even if he was aloof from others, was basically one of goodwill, though some questioned it because of the rough edges he occasionally exhibited. He never meant harm, but he had felt misunderstood more often than he liked, so working wood gave him an outlet for that frustration. Wood absorbed from his fingers, hands, even his whole body, all the tensions and sorrows he could not contain inside his own heart. Wood was one of the best friends he ever had. If it were not for trees, he'd be at a loss in this world. What would he otherwise do with his frustration, his pent-up energy or his creative need?

As he worked on the wood of the door for his family, he thought about his wife's tree poems. He liked them, but he'd rather sit quietly under a tree or sand the wood from some sacrificed limb than talk about trees. But her poems were good, and just as he knew he needed his outlet with his hands, he deeply understood how Sarah needed hers. Her creative hands left a mark not on solid wood but on the thinnest results of a tree: a thin pulp of eight-and-a-half-by-eleven wispy wood. He could almost see it floating in her hands with her poems giving him that same airborne sense. The words, which did not matter as much to him even if honed by her, always left him with that sense of floating.

He felt that way when he worked on her door—their door. It was as if he was floating through time, which was elusive and yet passing by too swiftly, time working against his desire to build a house. As he smoothed the wood of their family door, he hoped Julia would like it too. He could see his child moving in and out of the bottom half, playing just as Sarah had talked about from her childhood fantasy.

Tyler hoped the solid oak door would not overwhelm Sarah when he gave it to her, hoped her tears would not be too full, because he knew she would cry. He just prayed she would not weep so hard that it felt as if his heart would split in two. Then he felt unable to help her or hold her because he was so busy trying to put back together his own heart, so he could keep breathing. The pulse of life was at times just more than he could take. So his wood gave him the escape he needed from the emotions that swept too steadily into his life.

The door was true to form, with an oval cut out for a window, for the stained glass with a rose, which he had some while back asked Linnea to make. She knew how to create stained glass designs, and she knew about the door and Tyler's plans to hand carve it. She was looking forward to visiting Sarah after she had seen the door, on the Christmas to come in eight months time. Linnea was excited without thinking about the consequences of just how that door might affect her friend. It had not occurred to her that the door might be too much for Sarah, but Tyler knew it could be. He knew that when reality and fantasy meet, sometimes an abyss is created, and people fall through.

The oval hole in the door remained empty, but he had prepared it well for the stained glass. Its oval shape had been sanded over and over with the lightest of sandpapers and with the most gentle of touches. Ty knew this was the focal point of her Dutch door, which he planned to stain as close to a heather-toned finish as he could get. It would be darker than Sarah had described, because he knew the lovely oak pattern of the wood, in all its solidity and flow of grain, needed a darkened stain. For now he took pleasure in the pure blonde wood, a not-yet-stained wood that was smooth and soothing.

Tyler hoped his oak wood might grant them goodwill whenever they would come in and out of that front door. *That front door.* At least he had the door, but would he ever have the framework for the door, or a house where the framework would fit? He reminded himself he did have one huge step completed for their dream. Sarah did not know it yet, but Tyler had received word not long ago that a small piece of land had been left to him by his great aunt after her passing. It had been given to his great aunt by her grandfather, Professor Wolf, who in the 1800s had started a school in Pennsylvania before moving westward to Havener — or so Tyler was told in the will that named him the current landowner.

Unknown to Tyler, his great aunt Connie Dee had owned the property for years. The land consisted of three acres that was not farmable but stood between several farms. On it was Norris Creek, where Tyler had seen a sleek crane searching for fish when Ty had first gone to see what he had inherited. On a map he had hidden from Sarah, he learned the creek was a six-mile-long sliver of water. Three hundred feet of the creek made its way through his property, with trees hiding it from view. Most of the three acres were filled with trees, with a half-dirt, half-gravel road leading to it, also hidden by a few very old oaks and other younger oaks, and by cottonwoods, which loved the access to water. It was not what one would call ideal land and was unusable for nearby farmers, but it was more land than he had ever owned.

The land and door he would give as a surprise to Sarah and Julia. He planned to wrap with ornate paper a copy of the deed to the property and give it to Sarah.

The real title to the land was now locked up in a safety deposit box, unknown to her. When the time came he would surprise her. She'd open her gift of the title, and he would drive her to the new property in their old, reclaimed truck now dusty blue but which he planned to paint shiny red. He would buff and shine the candy apple red paint just for the occasion. He would clean the narrow rear window until it sparkled. He would make sure nothing could block the view out his long, rear view window so he'd be sure no one would see them drive to his secret property. He would blindfold Sarah as they drove closer to their land and let Julia give all the descriptive details of the ride to their land, as Julia was good at that kind of talking, just like her mother.

He would have the door, hinged on its proud frame, hidden among the trees resting against a tall, stately oak tree. He would take off her blindfold and surprise Sarah and Julia with the land and a promise of a house on their small property: land full of tall, living trees feeding off the creek, growing to their heart's content, ready to welcome a new home. Soon he would start clearing an area where he could build their house, which he hoped in a year or two he could begin to build, even if it took him some years to do it himself and to afford it. Yes, he'd start to clear his land in the summer after the door was complete, before his life became too complicated as it does when better weather brings extra carpentry projects. He would start the clearing of brush before he told Sarah about the land. Then he would bring her out and show her where their dream house would one day rest, proving to her he could make her happy in her own home.

It was not Tyler's job to bring Sarah happiness, but he did not know it. He was confused about how to love her, and in his misunderstanding was his turmoil. He was starting to weave a web that was tangling him in unexpected ways. He thought her happiness was his mission and Tyler was sure he could fulfill it. He was without any doubts that she would find happiness when he provided her a house to claim as her own.

10

Complexities

Sarah was concerned about how she would tell Tyler the news about Linnea getting the house. She was even more concerned about how he would react, for as rational as he could be, and as emotional as she was, he could be very reactive. It was that defensive reaction that concerned her, but Sarah knew he had to know, and soon because the newspaper would tell the story. She wanted him to hear it from her first, and she was glad Linnea and she had not yet told Julia or Blair about the house.

Even though it had not been that long since she had started helping Linnea with all the details of a house move, and there were so many particulars her head was swimming, Sarah felt awkward about not yet telling Tyler. She always confided in him even if her personal history took time to filter into their marriage. She liked honesty. She thought it kept the edges clean, the dust from piling up. "God so help me, I tell the truth," was for her a daily way of living. And she had not lied, but now it was time to clear off a bit of accumulated dust.

Tyler was soon to return from who knows where, as he was more secretive than usual. She had no qualms about his whereabouts, as she knew time had shown her he was as committed as anyone could be. His true colors came through because he always helped her whenever she was in a tough spot. He was there—all there—at those moments in time. She accepted his aloofness with assumptions he needed time either to roam or renew, so he had something left to give to her and Julia.

Sarah knew Linnea was planning a newspaper story about her house move, and it was to be printed the following week. However, unknown to both women, Linnea's father surprised everyone with front page coverage early. He was like that—he enjoyed being spontaneous and loved to surprise "the girls." Linnea and Sarah preferred to be called women, because as they said, how often were grown men called boys? But to Linnea's father they supposed they would always be "the girls," and so they put up with it, and loved him for his other endearing ways.

It was a great story with good photos, and the fascinating history of the Underground Railroad house was of an interest to many people in town. Linnea had called Sarah immediately when the article ran unexpectedly. She also told her a few people had since contacted her father with stories about their old house being part of the Underground Railroad, but with no proof, no written word as documentation, theirs was a history lost, even if truthful. On the whole the news article was well received, but because of the issue of teardowns dividing people, it had put more than one person, as they say, "up in arms."

Sarah thought "up in arms" was some colonial fighting term, a dated expression, but she had visions of people with arms flailing over their head, mad as heck. "Up in arms" should mean someone was picked up in another's arms and loved. Like the homeless around the world, or those who lay ill or distraught—should they not be helped? Sarah had heard of the dedicated work of compassionate people in India, and in America, and in many nations around the world. So many people and groups in different countries were trying to help and in growing numbers, and this inspired Sarah. Still she felt a sadness that homelessness was on the increase and in too many places.

Sarah thought it was a wrong state of affairs that more than one hundred million people around the world—a number difficult to comprehend—were homeless. How could that many people really be homeless? She had heard some folks in town talk about how it was the fault of the person who was homeless, but Sarah knew you could not blame one hundred million people. Sarah knew most homelessness had multiple causes which varied from country to country, yet many of the reasons shared certain commonalities between nations.

Sarah remembered when she learned mental illness was one of the major causes of homelessness in the United States. It made her think of her own mother who was pushed over the edge emotionally and suffered from mental illness. As a child Sarah assumed she and her mother were a rare few who were homeless and in difficult circumstances. As an adult she learned that long-term care institutions for those who were mentally ill were closed down, with the promise of halfway houses to be funded in the future. When government funding did not happen, homelessness increased with the majority of the homeless suffering from some type of mental illness. Sarah wondered how her life may have been different if her mother had been able to get help from the beginning of their problems. Learning about the causes of homelessness helped Sarah as an adult to realize it was not some fault of her own or her mother's. Sadly, as a child she had felt, like many children do, that the fault was her own.

Sarah thought her own country of birth, America, needed a visionary who would apply his or her compassionate values in ways to help others in great need. Then one of the wealthiest nations in the world could really be one of the richest, in spirit. Then the homeless of her own country could be helped with their problems, be it mental illness, lack of family support, or financial worries. Sarah knew a lack of job skills was one cause of homelessness. She also had read enough to know another cause was due to the lack of affordable housing. The more obvious problem, of people on the street because of substance abuse, Sarah had seen first hand when she was a child. As an adult Sarah knew it was as big a problem in homes behind closed doors.

When Sarah had read about post-traumatic stress for homeless veterans she better understood some of what she had witnessed in her youth. She recalled one of her mother's friends who suffered flashbacks. Sarah had observed the trauma first hand. Now as an adult, trying to understand her past and her current world, she was putting together the puzzle pieces. She was especially stunned to learn about the lack of help with transition from foster care into adult living after someone in a foster home turned eighteen years old. Only 180 dollars was given to such emancipated adults, and then they were on their own—a sure way, Sarah thought, to add to the homelessness in the world.

Truly helping people, that's what "up in arms" should be, Sarah pondered, lost in thought while waiting for Tyler to return. Up in arms meant to be carried, supported, and loved. Spirit had always taken her up in arms when she needed. She did not feel alone as long as she had wind and stars. She would imagine breathing in starlight and she'd "listen" while its quiet brilliance helped her feel soft and at peace. God had always wrapped her in a blanket of warmth, not in a church or even in a house for that matter, but inside her own self. A self that saw and felt and heard so much, hearing whispers of angels and ancient cultures singing songs of well-being if only a planet and its people would listen. Sarah listened and just wished more people could hear, of the goodness possible, of the light-filled place the earth could become.

She loved to contemplate a culture that would honor first the inherent integrity of all living life. She could imagine a different world; just as a child she could use her imagination to ascribe in her heart a true home, a world where love and integrity were the order of the day. Now Sarah realized she had to keep her mind on task. It had a way of running on with thoughts, but ideas and her imagination were her company and her good fortune because they kept her sane in an insane world. But the task at hand was her talking to Tyler, and he was coming through the door. She could tell he was angry. Much to her regret, Tyler had just found out the news before Sarah could go take him for a walk in her childhood woods and break it to him carefully.

He started right in: "Sarah, you deserve that house. If anyone does, you do! Did you see that newspaper article? How could Linnea think she should have the house? If Linnea is really such a good friend, why didn't she tell us about that house?"

"I know, Ty, but she needs a house. You know they lost their home, even before Ray died. She needs this," Sarah said firmly.

"She needs it more than we do? Does she deserve it more than you, Sarah? Linnea was never homeless like you. She has always had a home, one way or another. Her parents aren't exactly poor, you know."

"And they are not exactly rich either, Ty. You know her parents put up their house equity, taking a big risk, just so they could buy our small town newspaper. They could have lost everything. They worked very hard to make what they have today," Sarah said emphatically.

"I know the story, but what about you and what you have been through, how hard you've worked?" he asked resentfully.

On and on he went, with a spoken jealousy in which he didn't comprehend how he was setting himself up with his own limitations. But jealousy that is up front is much easier to deal with, Sarah thought, than the insidious, unspoken kind that ends up taking out anyone in its course and bears no insight. Sarah knew in the few times she had felt jealous pangs that it was time for self-reflection. And always it came back to the same issues: perception of lack or of limited ability. If one assumes one cannot get a house then one covets another's house. She had not ever done that; she never wished someone else did not have a home. She just wished she did.

And she knew God came through, maybe slowly at times, but lack was the creation of human beings. Lack was not of the spirit, unless it came as a spiritual lesson. So now she had to try to teach Tyler what she understood about abundance and lack, and she wanted to try to calm him down.

"Tyler, we will get our own house. Linnea found out about that one first and she needs it. She needs it more than we do. She's lost Ray. She can't have him back, but at least she can have the security of a home again," Sarah said with compassion.

Sarah's empathy was lost on Tyler. He was not happy to hear how much Sarah had already helped Linnea. When he heard that Linnea didn't even have the guts to ask Rolla and Grace Wolter herself, he was livid.

"How could she ask you to do that? Why would you agree to it, Sarah? I tell you, she's taking advantage of you and your good heart," he said angrily. Now he saw red, because he felt Sarah should never have been put in that position. He had forgotten that Sarah made all her own choices and lived by them well. She was happy and freed by helping Linnea. Tyler thought she was blind.

Tyler was not buying any of it. He should have been mad at Sarah, he had reason to be angry because she had not been honest, but instead he projected all his anger at Linnea. Sarah tried to console him and discuss how she was fine with it all, how she felt even closer to getting their own home than ever before, that she felt empowered in a way she had never before felt. Tyler would not hear it.

Their talk had gone worse than Sarah expected. She was relieved that Julia was gone, playing with Blair. She tried hard to keep adult complexities and conflicts from little ears. But at times they leaked through to childhood realities. She remembered in her own growing up the fights she heard and the confusion and fear they created in her. It was an odd world, Sarah thought, the adult world. She observed it then as a child and now as an adult with a sometimes childlike view. What was quite simple in life adults made complex. Rather than expressing their emotions, and then working it through to find solutions like she always attempted with people close to her, most adults she knew held on to their assumptions and judgments, and thus complexities ensued. From Sarah's perspective, such judgments kept them from the simplicity inherent in life. Now she had to work harder at helping Tyler see her reality, but that would not be simple.

Freedom

Sarah had been distressed ever since the day Tyler and she had talked about Linnea's house move. Sarah knew she needed perspective, so she drove their old blue truck alone for one of her country drives. She needed to think and to understand more about her life and how it fit into a larger picture. She decided to drive west out of town to the back roads full of cornfields starting to grow, with a rich earthy scent, so she could reflect and get a better perspective.

On her drive past old farm houses and the green of everything growing, Sarah started reflecting upon that elusive quality called freedom: freedom to make choices about a home, or about one's emotional response. Although still upset by Tyler's reaction, she didn't want to think about him or their conflict, so she put both out of her thoughts. She had learned long ago how to cope in this way.

The word "freedom" hung in her mind as the intensity of it sounded within her like a huge but soft ringing bell. She knew freedom was part of the cause of her father's desire to immigrate. He had given up much of his own history and heritage for freedom's respite, as do many immigrants who sacrifice so that something new in their individual pathway or their family's journey may be born. For her father the sacrifice meant his heritage would not remain as he knew it. His family abandoned him because they could not bear his separation, not in miles but in decorum and deference. For him the freedom to make his own choices apart from familial or societal expectations was worth the act of severing ties, even his promised inheritance. He longed for the unknown and the new, for a freedom to be his own person, but it came at a huge cost.

Without his past heritage, given like tokens to the multiple gods of loss, he could only make a beginning. So his family lineage went forward into the future. He could not know it then, but through his daughter he was helping to create a different world, a more just and healed place of which she was becoming one creative voice of many in a song resonant with possibility. Yes, Sarah's father had given mightily, without understanding all the loss it would entail, or the gain, for freedom's sake and for his daughter's future.

Driving the open road helped Sarah to think. The expanse of farmland and open blue sky dotted with full, white clouds helped her go more deeply into her thinking. Sarah thought freedom to be an elusive quality, and yet a force so powerful, it pulls of its own accord. It was the drawing force of those escaping slavery, those who chanced their very lives to know the potential that freedom held for them.

Sarah had wondered, how many freedom seekers made it to their promised land? Canada had become that land of freedom after the passing of the Fugitive Slave Act of 1850 in an America that ruled any person escaping or any person helping someone escape in both the south and in the north would be severely punished by law. That severity included a thousand-dollar fine — an enormous amount of money back then, as Sarah had learned. Sarah had researched and discovered that anyone escaping or assisting could also be thrown in jail for six months. It was an unjust law aimed at stopping the Underground Railroad in its tracks. Yet it only served to fuel the movement of whites and blacks cooperating together to end slavery.

Sarah contemplated the number of people who had been caught trying to escape slavery, only to be recaptured in the chains of an oppressive world. Freedom was worth one's very breath of life. People escaping slavery, strong freedom seekers grabbed it whenever they could, holding on to freedom's ring for dear life. Sarah knew from her studies that many people did reach freedom in Canada, to create lives of their own making, as free as was possible at that time in history. Free to educate their children. Free to earn and keep a wage. Free to own property if they could find a way to buy it. Those were precious freedoms to a people once enslaved by others who were bereft of empathy.

Sarah was aware that Chicago was a main route to Canada by way of the boats heading north off Lake Michigan. If freedom seekers could make it to Chicago and to the boats, then freedom was closer at hand. Illinois had multiple Underground Railroad stops and Sarah had been fascinated to learn in school about its complex, if painful history. Sarah also came to understand that the Underground Railroad had its limitations because many times people once held as slaves had to hide without a safe home because one was not nearby, and still so many freedom seekers took the risk. Often the only place for hiding was a woods by a river that lead north, with trees that gave a guiding path because of the moss that grew on the north side of trees trunks.

Freedom felt less elusive now to Sarah as she reflected upon the risks taken, the punishments suffered and lives forsaken because freedom had its call. People escaping slavery exemplified the inner call to freedom. Her own father had risked everything, even if not equal to the loss of a people enslaved, so he could be freer to make his own way. Freedom would always have its call, Sarah realized, and one of the reasons the stories of immigrants or the Underground Railroad movement held such fascination was because at some visceral level many understood that call: the sometimes lone echo of the call of freedom.

In understanding that call, Sarah felt a reverence for the ring of freedom, and felt a respect to all those who walked before on its path, whatever their sacrifice. Freedom seekers, be they from slavery in America or centuries of immigrants, understood the basics of true freedom: the freedom of worship, the freedom to be educated, the freedom of speech, the freedom to be treated fairly, and the important freedom to choose those governing.

These were just and good causes. But Sarah thought freedom was far more than those concrete and sometimes elusive qualities supported in a democracy. They were real enough in democratic nations, and valuable, for a world without such basic freedoms leads only to more despair, and additional wounds and losses. Yet there was more to freedom, she knew. It was this growing edge, of freedom in a land of many immigrants, of searching souls wanting something greater that motivated Sarah to expand her concept.

While taking in the beauty of nature on her roaming roads and leaving behind all her worldly problems, Sarah started to think about freedom as having an inner ring. Sarah rarely heard it mentioned but she knew freedom had an inner calling, a new way of being in the world.

For Sarah, freedom meant she had clear reign in her thinking and her expression. She knew if she could change her thinking she was free. Freedom also meant she had time: free time to explore and learn and think as only her mind worked, in its uniqueness. Freedom meant she could spend quiet time reflecting while in nature, with the natural world honored by her in that walk of contemplation. Freedom also meant to be freed of others judgments or misperceptions, being free to know one's own esteem as meaningful.

Yet most vital for Sarah was the freedom to rest in the quiet place inside her own soul, where she was at peace. Within her prayerful quietness, she discovered a place of sanctity she knew as sheer freedom.

Without discounting other aspects of it, Sarah knew freedom for her was very personal and internal. Maybe she was able to search more deeply because she came from immigrant heritage. Possibly it was because more than fifty years had transpired since people in the subcontinent of India in search of freedom from English domination took hold of their freedom and she viscerally understood this as part of her heritage. Maybe it was because the slaves of America who suffered inhumanities became freedom seekers and lead the path to an inner knowing of freedom, one she shared in a new century. Maybe it was because those with certain freedoms today were seeking for something greater within a democracy, as was she.

Freedom — which had felt so tenuous when she first thought about it on her country drive — seemed apparent to Sarah. Because of the many people who lived before her she had the freedom to consider such creative ideas. She knew of her parent's sacrifices, and of her great-grandfather in Chittigong, who followed an uncommon career in medicine. She knew clearly of the freedom seekers who took risk after risk, and of Grace Wolter's relatives who also took chances. It took great empathy and courage for people from the nineteenth century to take a stand against slavery. Thinking about empathy as Sarah drove on the open land that for centuries had been sacred to American Indians, whose freedom and rights she knew had been stripped from them, Sarah realized empathy for others gave her a deep sense of freedom. This was another one of the new bells of her sacred freedom, one with empathy and compassion as its vibrating call.

Sarah was a freedom seeker at the turn to the twenty-first century, and her road to freedom was within. It was because of all the risk takers who walked before her that she could take freedom to a new level, to an inner depth that gave freedom a whole new ring. External freedom she knew needed the balance of inner freedom or its true meaning was lost. In that realm of discovery of the inner world, Sarah was a wise leader, and without her knowing it yet, she was part of the essence of a larger discovery being made by many in America, her nation of birth and by many in India, her nation of heritage, and by people all over the world.

A movement was afoot, an inner movement with sacred freedom as its beckoning call. Sarah was a part of that impulse for a better and a more sacred world, and the sacrifices made by her father and mother would prove worthy, for Sarah was part of something far larger than her small town sphere.

With her new thoughts coming together during her ride westward, she decided it was time to head back home. She knew her husband was angry, and she would have to use as much empathy as she could to understand him and help him expand his own perceptions. She knew she had a task ahead in continuing to help Linnea get her Underground Railroad house moved. She also knew she wanted to focus on getting her own house, after Linnea's project was completed, because she thought she had the confidence now to make it happen. Once again the long country drive on Midwestern soil helped her to answer her philosophical questions, be they about freedom or history, and to gain enough perspective to carry on.

12

Leroy and Binnie

Sarah had first met the elderly couple at the town library after a lecture had been given there about local history. The three of them immediately took a liking to one another and a friendship for some years had developed. On a few special occasions, Sarah had been to their house for a good home cooked meal, invited by Binnie because she knew Sarah needed an extra something. Binnie became a kind of female mentor without either of them thinking about it as such. Leroy became the storyteller and the humorist who always got both women to laughing.

The three of them developed an unspoken bond, partly because they each had faced discrimination of one kind or another, and in part because they shared a similar understanding about the world that kept them in one another's confidence. Binnie knew about Sarah's past homelessness more than anyone and Sarah knew as an inter-racial couple Binnie and Leroy had been put through their share of difficulties.

Leroy was a black man who had come up from the South in 1961 to Havener, and he was the love of Binnie's life. They had met when both were in their late twenties. It did not take long for them to have the other one clearly figured out and to know theirs was a match if ever there was one. Binnie would have done anything to marry him and live out their days together, and time had shown their commitment had made their vision worthy. Leroy felt the same love in return for Binnie, and when he was fully determined to make something happen, it was as good as done. Theirs was the kind of love too rare in marriage and it deserved its due respect.

Binnie fell in love with this tall, large black man who had a presence that stretched full out when he entered a room, filling it up with his unique goodwill and a smile that encompassed every person around him. He also had a certain solitude about him that gave a person pause. People who knew him well enough had a sense of his warmth, and a measure of his goodness but respected that he was a private man. His favorite time was being alone, enjoying the view of the sun setting on his fields, which had been well cared for by him for many years, along with Binnie who had been his partner right beside him making their farm function.

Leroy had faired better when he moved up north to Havener, though of course he always stood out in their small town. Because of the good reputation he earned due to his farm work, it helped many people transcend issues of racism. Leroy and Binnie had been skilled farmers and had well earned the respect of people in the area who worked the land. Leroy was the kind of person who could get almost anything to grow gloriously. He had in his hands that magic of a good farmer, and he taught Binnie some of his gardening secrets, secrets he thought might go back generations to Africa. He thought this was an interesting idea, like the many he contemplated while in the solitude of country living, knowing that he and Binnie were a part of the land on which they depended.

So when Sarah suddenly saw Leroy and Binnie,

with each one knowing of the other's complicated history, they were more than glad to see one another. She had been heading back home after another one of her drives on country roads, and while coming up to their house she saw them in their truck pulling into their farm. She waved and then pulled in behind them and got out of her vehicle to greet them.

"Sarah, how nice to see you," Binnie said, giving her a hug.

"And you. Hi, Leroy," Sarah said warmly.

"Hello, child. Are you out for a country drive? There's no better day for one," he said as he kissed her soft cheek.

"Yes, I was driving, trying to collect my thoughts. There's a lot going on with the house move," she told them.

"So we hear. We have not seen you much, so you will have to catch us up," Binnie requested.

"Well, Linnea and I have been working hard to get things going. She did get the house given to her, by Grace and Rolla, for one dollar," she explained.

"Imagine a dollar for a house, hm, hm," said Leroy, slowly shaking his head in disbelief.

"They're glad we are saving it from being torn down," Sarah stated.

"And so are we. We have heard stories about that house for years as being part of the Underground Railroad. Then people say you can't prove it," said Binnie.

"Grace Wolter has a diary from her great-great-grandmother who writes about the Underground Railroad, so this house has documentation," Sarah was glad to say.

"It was a difficult time for my people. Some days I can still see the lasting influences from slavery and its long aftermath. It's good there was a "railroad of the heart" as I like to call it. Just think how much more people would have suffered back then, without the Underground," he said reflectively.

"People shouldn't have had to suffer in slavery," Sarah acknowledged.

Leroy knew of this struggle with racism too often as a boy growing up. He recalled once when a teacher tried to tell his mother on his first day of school that he could not learn to read early, even though he was reading steadily by that time. He remembered his best friend, who was black, was once told as a child that he was not very smart. This friend later went to medical school and became a doctor. "You proved her wrong," Leroy had once said to him. "Just plain wrong."

"Yes, too much suffering and not enough laughing, as your mama always said," Binnie added.

"You and me, we brought in more laughter, didn't we honey?" he said, as he put his arm around her.

Nowadays no one much bothered them, because in a culture that glorified youth and had little left of shock value, their inter-racial marriage was no longer a focus. Binnie had even told Sarah once that she liked being older as a woman, because it was like wearing camouflage. Since she went unnoticed by many in a country that narrowed its focus on youthfulness, she could be all the more observant, as if she could invisibly walk in the world while witnessing everything around her. And such observing had taught her a lot about people. She had such a knowing way about her, as if just from her silences, let alone her spoken wisdom, one could write books.

"Everything okay with you both?" Sarah asked in her giving way.

"Oh, yes. Just watching the fields and the sunrises," said Leroy with his loving smile.

"And the sunsets," added Binnie, as if reminding them they were in their twilight years.

Sarah loved this older couple who had taken her under their wing and become like family. She admired their wisdom gained from many life experiences and a history of facing their own troubles. She was reluctant to take leave of them but knew she had to get back to her family and be prepared to help Linnea with her house move.

"I wish I could stay longer but I have to get back, I've been driving for quite awhile. I'll keep you posted on our progress," Sarah promised.

"Please do. We would love to hear about your house adventures," Binnie emphasized.

"One question before you go, Sarah. How is it you're not taking the house for a dollar? Seems with you having been homeless, well, maybe it's your due," Leroy asked directly.

"I would only tell you two this. I would love to have the house, but it's just not meant to be. Linnea seems to need this more than me after all she has been through. I'm her best friend, so I decided I'd help her. And I feel more confident now it will lead me to a house of my own," Sarah replied.

"Well, then, if you're sure, we wish you well," Leroy said, as he accepted her honest answer.

"We'll see you soon, we hope. And don't you worry, Sarah, you'll get a house someday," said Binnie. "I think we'll take our walk now. Dusk isn't too far off and it's our favorite time for a stroll." She added, "Drive safe, darling," while Sarah hugged her goodbye.

Binnie and Leroy started their walk hand-in-hand by the side of their cornfields. Some old stalks rustled with the unmistakable sound only corn stalks can make in a prairie wind. They loved their corn and their wildflowers and prairie plants on the roadsides, and both loved their evening walks. Even as they grew older they took to walking whenever weather permitted. On this particular evening they stopped along the way to look at their favorite flower, Queen Anne's lace, and for that moment they delighted in the rich, darkest of purples in the center surrounded by the delicate and creamy lace pattern of the flower.

"There is dark and there is light, not so opposite. Just a nice contrast," said Binnie as she looked at the flower of black-purple and creamy white.

"You are sugar, white sugar, and I'm dark brown sugar, and together, we are sweet as honey," Leroy told her.

As her older friends took their walk while dusk quickly approached, Sarah continued her journey home, thinking about what Leroy had asked her. She had not let herself fully admit to wanting the house until she had told them aloud she would have liked it. She was accustomed to not owning much, but it was nice to fantasize about the house being for her family. What would it feel like to have someone give you a whole house, she wondered? She felt conflicted about wanting the house because she knew it was Linnea's idea, and she knew her friend wanted it in almost a desperate way. Sarah decided right then and there that Linnea needed it far more than she did. As she drove back to town, Sarah told herself to put aside her imagination about the Underground Railroad house being her own. All she had to do, she told herself, was to stay in touch with the insights she was discovering on her country drives and then she could stay the course. She just hoped she could let go entirely of her hidden desire, while handling her resentful husband, and be ready for whatever next steps were needed in helping Linnea with house moving.

13

A House Moving Plan

Linnea had always been good at developing and following through with a plan. A skilled researcher, she had intensely thrown herself into learning everything she could about house relocation. She absorbed all of it diligently; studying, taking copious notes, and plotting all the intricacies of her house moving plans. There was so much at stake. She and Blair needed this house, a home in which to surrender and heal, so Linnea had to learn all she could.

"This is a major undertaking," her father told her.

"I know, but I think I'm up to the challenge," Linnea responded.

"You sure you want to do this?" he asked.

"Dad, I'm sure. We need a place—we can't keep living with you and Mom," Linnea stated.

"We just want to be certain it's not too much for you," her father confessed. But he knew how resourceful his daughter had always been, so he didn't say more.

She was resourceful, having long ago found within herself an inner well, a place of sound resilience. It was a corner of her soul, which kept her afloat in life when nothing else worked. It was what helped her cope with the drawn-out death of her husband, a death that had taken far too long because of his suffering. Yet those last hours, when the end was finally upon them, had seemed sudden to her. How could she be prepared for what she kept pushing away? She had felt time slipping through her hands as if her fingers were sieves in those final hours of his death. She had no hold on him. All she could feel was him slipping from her as she was vividly aware of all the years stolen from them. A thief had come and taken year upon year from them as a couple and from their parenting of Blair. Linnea could hardly acknowledge the pain for her daughter because she herself could not bear the loss Blair and she would always know.

On those days when she was softened by her pain, Linnea could almost believe Ray might be watching over Blair and her now. She remembered hearing Sarah say Ray was "pulling strings up there" just so Blair and Linnea could get the house. Linnea, being a rational woman, did not subscribe to the same spiritual views as did Sarah, but over the years she had come to respect the wisdom that was hidden beneath Sarah's surprising words. Sarah would come up with a phrase that made complete sense to Linnea, at least in the moment, even if it did not subscribe to Linnea's logic. Other times, they had very different world views, with Linnea the logical one and Sarah the intuitive one. But soul-linked the women remained because their world was large enough for them to see God, ideas, and earthly events from differing vantage points. Their friendship was deeper than personal beliefs. They lived in daily ways a sense of connectedness and love to which religions ascribed. They knew it with ease and grace and without pretense. It was the creation of a bond that bore the fruits of the spirit and the generousness of their flexibility.

It was a blessing for the moment that Linnea was the logical and practical one, for that down-to-earth side had to be in full gear now as she worked on all the details of moving a house. Her planning helped her to stay focused on all things logical. She had to communicate with all the utility companies and set them up for house moving day. Numerous phone calls had to be made to the electric company with plans to move the electric wires overhead on several streets on the big day. Almost as many calls had to go to the phone company so they could make their plans to unhook or drop their wires when the house moved down the street.

Unlike the past when houses were moved, these days there were fiber optic lines owned by cable companies, the thick black lines low down on the telephone poles. The cable company, Linnea had found out, does not like to cut their fiber optic wires because it affects the current running through them, so they have loops in the long lengths of cables which they pull from quite a distance, from street block after street block, to get enough slack. On moving day the plan would be to drop the wires, cover them with steel plate runners, and let the house just wheel over them. But that slack had to be prepared many days in advance, so it also had to be set up prior to moving day.

Then there was the financial end of her plan. All the contracts had to be signed for the cable company, the phone, and the electric. Risk money had to be put forward as a down payment. It was a calculated risk, but house moving is a risk none the less, just as chances are taken in any building project. Linnea had learned the risk was far less than most people realized as long as the house mover was competent, and almost all were, except for one or two bad apples which all the rest of the movers more than disliked. One story was of an incompetent house mover and a house he moved but dropped on its side when two wheels on one end of the house passed over very soft ground. That soft soil might as well have been quicksand, as it was just enough to tilt the house so that it fell over in ruin. There also was the story of a house being hit by a train while crossing the railroad track, but today house moving was much better planned when it moved over the tracks. Train tracks fortunately were not a concern with Linnea's house move. She had wires and trees and financing to contend with but no trains. She was thankful for her blessings. She also knew her house mover was competent, as her mover, Everett, had never lost a house.

Money was found for her entire project from a loan. She had met a banker who was willing to take a risk on her and her project once they calculated that the value of the house would exceed by forty percent the cost of the whole project. That was a day, Linnea told Sarah, she would never forget.

"Sarah, you won't believe what I just found out. I never imagined this being part of the deal. I have good news—no, I have great news," she said.

"What is it? Tell me," she said like a co-conspirator. "Did you get two houses?" Sarah teased, still in some disbelief about one house for free.

"Not two, no, but I can't believe what I just found out. You know I have to borrow to pay the house mover, and all the lines that have to be lifted, dropped, or unhooked on house moving day, they all have their cost. And there is the whole new foundation, which adds a big chunk of money, then money for hook-up to the street for water and sewer, and gas and new electric to the house once it is in place. Then there's the cost for the renovation, though the house is in pretty good shape." Linnea was stalling in telling Sarah her news.

"I know. It's a house that has been taken care of by many people, including me," Sarah reflected. Her tender ways in helping the previous owners of the home had become part of the mystery in those walls, in the way a house soaks up good intent. "It's in very good shape. You will just have to paint walls and sand the wood floors. You won't have to strip the wood trim around the doors and windows of paint because the Wolter's had sense enough to not paint their window trim. And it is oak; I asked. Lucky you! Remember when we stripped white paint off that rocking chair? What a chore that was!"

"That rocker gave us some trouble, but at least you have a solid chair." She paused. "Well, you won't believe it. I feel kind of uncomfortable telling you this, but I will have a lot of equity in the house once I am done, at least forty percent. I had to sit down when I realized it. But that is also why I can get the loan, besides the value of the land. That house's financial value will be higher than what I have to spend, even allowing for run-over costs. Can you believe it?" said Linnea.

"Well, I can. I just knew this was meant to be. You deserve it, Linnea, after what you and Blair have been through. I'm happy for you, I really am," said Sarah. She felt true joy for her friend even if she felt more aware of a emptiness in her own life.

Linnea knew her friend meant it; she was happy for her. She secretly hoped she could soon turn around and help Sarah get a house. Maybe she could use some of her house equity for a down payment on a house for Sarah. She would do it for Sarah, she promised herself, because of their friendship, because of Sarah's willingness to give.

But to get to that place of abundance Linnea had to focus and achieve a great deal in a short time. She had spent a lot of time already talking to Everett, discussing with him the articles about house relocation she had researched, reading many publications about house moving, as many as she could find in her research. There were very few books but she did find one she had ordered from a library as far away as Oregon. They helped answer many of her house moving questions.

The rest of her questions she had asked of her house mover, who seemed both humored and attentive as he answered her. He seemed to care about her project and about the old house without showing it much. To demonstrate it overtly would have gone against his manner, but he did care and she sensed it. It was good to feel that a contractor could care for more than just a job well done, but also for the long-term outcome of saving a house. He was aware of how his work would support this small, vulnerable family in need and he was pleased he could help.

"My father liked helping folks get a house. You know, Dad used to move houses on wood beams only, not steel. He said he could tell what was happening with the house as it moved, just by listening to the sound of wood on wood. Kinda like a good mechanic knows an engine from hearing sounds," Everett said.

"That's something, that your father had the skill to decipher the sounds of wood on wood," said Linnea.

"He was a good old house mover. He taught me about wood beams and those creaks, but these days we movers tend to use steel. No matter what, these old houses move well. They don't make houses today like they used to," he said.

"No, they sure don't," Linnea answered. "I think the old Underground Railroad house is built solid. I love those black walnut beams you showed me when we looked at the foundation."

"It's interesting to see how they built way back then. It will be a good home for you. Maybe someday your daughter will be able to leave it to her children, if she stays in your small town," he said.

"I hope one day this house gets passed down generation to generation. Just think—she could be mortgage free!" Linnea responded, wondering why more people didn't keep their homes and pass them down to help the next generation.

She enjoyed talking to Everett. In some of her conversations with him, Linnea had found out more about the history of structural moving, going back to ancient Egyptian times. He had shared some of his research showing that most house moving had been done in the United States and Canada in the nineteenth and twentieth century. He did show her a picture of a structure in Pennsylvania that was moved vertically up a steep hillside, which Linnea had said was hard to believe. A newspaper he gave her told of an old movie theater in New York that moved from one end of the block to the other on top of railroad tracks laid down to move the structure. But Linnea was especially amazed with a conversation they had about two house moves.

"Yes, they move houses on barges these days. You can see pictures on the Internet. There is one of a company that moved three houses together on one barge…it's cheaper if you move them together," Everett explained.

"It must be incredible to see houses moving across water," Linnea said, surprised.

"It is. The move I liked was the Zook house and studio. That one takes the cake. Zook was a well known Chicago architect at one time. Now he's gone, but his house in Hinsdale, here in Illinois, was going to be torn down. That town has lost a lot of well-built houses from quality wood to the tear down craze. Well, several large donations later and many people helping, the Zook house and his studio were saved and moved. A mover I know had to split it apart into four sections, move all four loads separately down neighborhood streets over a three day period…it took longer than expected. He moved it to the Katherine Legge Memorial Park, on County Line Road if you want to see it, and then he and his crew had to put it all back together again," Everett told her.

"I wish I'd seen that house move," Linnea stated, trying to imagine four sections in transit.

She was excited when she discovered the early nineteen hundreds were full of house moving projects in her own area. She had talked to local people and heard about horses pulling houses on long, cut logs set underneath the house used for rolling it down the street. As the house moved slowly, the last log freed would then be carried up front. It was a continuous cycle of wood logs and a wooden house in motion.

She knew past methods of moving with horse and logs had long been replaced by trucks, steel beams, and unified hydraulic jacking systems so to ensure a house stays level. Gauges in the system keep the house mover attuned to the house so it always remains level while it is being set on steel beams because a house must be level to prevent structural damage. The technology of the system had real benefits. Still, if a house could be moved in the past without such technology and hold up, even moved by logs and horses, then Linnea thought it showed how sturdy and well made the old houses were and how skilled the movers were.

In her planning she had talked to the woman who worked for the railroad whose sole job was to be in charge of all the house moves across the railroad tracks in the Midwest. This was when one possible house route involved the tracks. Linnea was amazed to learn there were so many house moves across the rails. She had no idea there was a whole network of people who moved houses or attended to house moves.

But now that she was going to move her house, she was glad the network existed because she had found many people who were willing to talk to her and share their knowledge. And as hard as it was for her to believe, she learned more than ten thousand structures were moved or lifted for putting in new foundations every year. Knowing this meant she was not alone.

Linnea had also learned trimming trees often was part of the move, and so she had contacted her local town arborist to see if any trees would be affected. She lined that up as well, though for her house move tree trimming would not be significant until she came closer to her lot. Because the house was not very tall, tree trimming along her route would be minimal. Lucky for her there were no street lamps that had to be moved, just one stop light would have to be swung out of the way. And of course the police would have to escort the house and block the roads and be a helpful presence on house moving day.

Linnea and Sarah had put so much into their plan and their efforts for the house move to go smoothly. It was a full-time job to prepare for everything, be it obtaining road permits, checking various contracts, handling the bank financing, turning in the architectural foundation drawings to her village, complete with topographical drawings from a civil engineer, lining up the contractors for the foundation to be poured, and on and on and on.

Linnea loved the learning curve and all the planning of such a large event. Everything in her life was intense as she lived, ate, and breathed "house move." It was the consummate adrenalin rush. Nothing yet had compared to this, not even critical newspaper deadlines. Planning a house move was the busiest she had ever been. Since she worked for her parents, who understood her needs, she was given flexibility with her hours, which was a great relief to her. She was also relieved she had a friend like Sarah who helped with Blair and who was willing to help with the complex house moving plans. She would always be grateful for such a loyal friend. She knew her daughter was in safe hands and that her own sacrificed time in mothering now would benefit her child later because they would have a home.

She also knew she could count on her mover to do his job. Linnea realized it took a certain kind of man who has the mental capacity to move an entire house. Everett was one of those men. She and Sarah had watched him move another house so they would be better prepared when their day came. He had been working with a second mover on a big project: taking a large old house, three stories high with a ballroom on the third floor, over what had been cornfields, across a road, and back over another cornfield to its new location.

The day they drove out to watch, they were amazed at what they witnessed: a huge house set on beams and with surprisingly small wheels attached to those beams. The plan was for those wheels to move on landing gear—long metal pieces usually used for planes to land on grass surfaces or deserts—but now the gear was set down on an unseeded cornfield. Placed on hardened soil, the runners were lined up by the crew, ready for the house on wheels to make its journey to a new resting place. Very slowly the huge house began to move. As they watched it, they had to study the house carefully, realizing they must look at it in relationship to something on the horizon in order to see that the house was actually moving. It was that slow going, but they did see it move for several hours through unseeded farmland and across the road. It was Sarah who started the conversation.

"Can you believe this?" she said with awe.

"You know I can't. But there it is…it's a massive house. After all the reading I have done on house moving, nothing compares to seeing the real thing," said Linnea as she stared at the house.

"You are definitely in the best of hands with this house mover," Sarah emphasized.

"If he can move that huge house across the empty cornfields, then he can move my much smaller house down the street. I've just let go of my last worries," said Linnea, with relief in her voice.

On that note they stood in silence, as if standing before something sacred. Both were mesmerized with the skills of the movers and their capacity to relocate a huge old house. With the soft heat surrounding the beauty of a late spring day, marked by sunlight and the shade of an old house on the move, Sarah and Linnea stood steadfast in the friendship that bonded them since childhood, awestruck by a huge old house on the move and contemplating their house moving day yet to happen.

14

House Raising

Linnea and Sarah met at the site of the 1853 house with the house mover and his crew, a place linking current people to a distant yet relevant past. They knew this was the time they would have the thrill of seeing how the Underground Railroad house would be raised and lifted off its foundation. The old stone of the foundation walls had withstood nearly 150 years, until this day, when it would succumb to a crumbled fate. At least the house would be saved, soon to be rising and on its way to a new adventure.

"I've read about how a house is prepared, but seeing is believing. This is a day I've been looking forward to for some time," Linnea said in a satisfied manner.

"You can say that again," added Sarah.

"You would think more people would be interested in this part of the move, in all the preparation. I find this just as interesting as the actual move down the street," Linnea said.

"I just want to know how they raise the whole house off its foundation. You've been secretive about this part. How do they lift the house off that big hole of a basement in the ground?" Sarah asked.

"You'll see. I want to keep it a surprise. This will be something to watch. We will have to bring the girls by later to show them," said Linnea.

"Julia keeps asking, 'Is the house in the air yet, Mommy?'" said Sarah, smiling.

"I'm sure both girls will wonder how such a big, heavy house can be moved. Everett says it takes about three days to prepare the house for the move," Linnea said.

"This is something to see, that's for sure," responded Sarah. "I'm so glad I'm here."

"I'm glad, too," Linnea said, feeling thankful she wasn't alone.

Sarah started thinking about how she could have ended up somewhere other than Havener, Illinois. Suddenly she had a flashback memory of her homelessness, which jarred her current equilibrium. She recalled a time when she and her mother had walked near a highway: the distance seemed endless. She remembered how tired her little legs felt. They found a place to sleep under a concrete bridge that had an opening like a cave. In order to keep out of the rain they and a few other homeless people were hidden, all of them hearing the rush of cars as people drove by fast under or over the bridge. The traffic sound was intrusive in its constancy, and Sarah tried to tell her mother she did not like it, but her mother could not hear her sad statements for reasons other than the noise.

They lived under that bridge for a few weeks until the authorities finally came and made them leave. That is when a police officer asked them both to come with him, and her mother complied. It was that officer, who had been kind to Sarah and who discovered that she was not yet school educated. Sarah was already nine years old and starting an education at age six was the law in America. That incident started the changes in her life, and was the moment in time when she was first separated from her mother. After it became apparent that her mother could not care for her, a home was found for Sarah with Linnea and her family.

Sarah felt relief now that she had not remained homeless, even though she still felt sad about losing her mother. As she stood before the old historical house she realized just how far she had come in her life. Although the sadness over the loss of both of her parents always remained, she was grateful another family had taken her into their hearts. She was also glad she had a family of her own, which she had chosen to create.

She was relieved to be in the present moment, to be standing in front of a house that once again was part of history in the making. It was good to be involved with such an interesting house — even if it was not meant to be her home. She also knew that some day, in whatever way it might unfold for her, she would also own a home and claim it as her own. Knowing this would happen helped her to stop thinking of the hurtful past and focus on the here and now, observing the house movers as they started to work on Linnea's old house.

Everett had been moving houses ever since he was a boy learning from his father. House moving was one of the last arts handed down from father to son. At the age of seven, Everett went on his first house move with his father, watching and even taking an order or two. Every summer he assisted his Dad with many house moves. Knowledge, experience, and the handling of equipment were all part of a good house mover's background, and Everett's father had taught him well.

After many house moves with his dad he developed the mindset and the skills so he was able to move multiple tons of someone's dream home. At least six hundred structures had been moved with Everett and his father working together and independently over many years.

They had made a difference with six hundred structures that were saved and continued in their usefulness.

Everett's first task with Linnea's house was to pound large holes into designated spots in the upper foundation walls. This would allow an opening for the steel beams to be inserted with the help of heavy equipment and the small number of men in his crew. They planned to push the beams through the holes in the foundation walls and set them at key points of contact under the wooden house. The beams would hold the structural weight of the historic house once it was resting on top of the metal beams.

"We're done pounding holes in the old foundation, and ready to inset the I-beams. We'll swing them around and set them under the house," Everett told her.

"I see the guys under there setting up the cribbing and getting ready for the beams," answered Linnea.

"Cribbing looks like building with Lincoln Logs, but those railroad ties are heavy. We'll have her rolled off that foundation and have her ready to move, right on schedule," he assured her.

"You movers obviously know what you're doing. We'll stay back and watch the steel beams go under my house," Linnea told him.

Those steel I-beams were familiar to both women from seeing them at many commercial building sites. Linnea knew once the house was lifted upon the beams, with shims to adjust it, that the solid steel would keep the house level. To ensure this critical leveling factor, the house, with its hydraulic jacking system, was hooked up to dozens of dials for reading the level of the house as it was lifted. Linnea had already explained to Sarah that good movers ensure against structural damage because they know how to prevent it, which was a comfort to both women.

Everett knew just how to work with the house, and

with the shims and the adjustments. As he and his crew did their tasks the house was prepared to be lifted ever so slowly by small hydraulic jacks set on wooden piers stacked up as cribbing in various places under the house. It was these small but powerful jacks that were set on the stable cribbing that would inch the house upward. The house had to be raised enough so that it could then be rolled off the old foundation.

So during those three clear days in May with no one present except the house mover, a crew, and two risk-taking women, the house was prepared and ready to begin its first movements. It was as if the house with the history that once had secretly hidden people on the move toward freedom was now set for its own motion. Slowly, the house began to rise; both women were thrilled.

"Sarah, did you ever imagine we would be standing here, watching this?" asked Linnea.

"You know, more than most people, I never would have thought so. But today it seems the impossible is possible," Sarah answered.

"I've had some wild ideas," Linnea said, shaking her head.

"And this one beats them all," Sarah said, smiling.

They stood before the humble but solid house as it kept rising off the foundation walls, suspended as if it was hovering. Sarah thought guidance from above must be helping such a feat. She imagined those who had lived or passed through the house were now standing guard, protecting it. In her imagination freedom seekers from another century were holding prayer vigils in heaven as gratitude for a house that once had kept them hidden and safe on their road to freedom. She thought they would have wanted the unique house saved as a reminder of the good in people and of the need for freedom. With heaven bound guardians in her mind's eye, Sarah also imagined angels observing, guiding, and protecting the house and watching over everyone involved with saving it.

Linnea, not one for "the imaginary" as she called it, kept watching Everett. She thought he was the one who would get her house safely to a new location. She felt a deep respect for this man who had the mindset to be able to move an entire house, as well as the guts to do it. Only so many men would ever take on the challenge of moving houses that weigh tons, defying gravity a bit, or at least teasing it. Everett was one of the rare men who had received the skills of his father before him, and thus the mentoring of those abilities. He was also one of the few left who was good for his word. If he agreed to something it was as good as a contract. Of course, contracts were always signed but there was no small print that was difficult to decipher. In a world too full of empty words and false promises, his type was a dying breed.

It reminded Linnea of stories about her great-great-grandfather, George Warder Hunley, who was also a man of his word. Her grandmother had told her that George put himself through business college, and then he became a teller in a small bank in Garnett, Kansas. He steadily bought stock over the years in the bank until he owned nearly half the stocks, and then the primary owner decided to sell him the rest. So George Hunley moved up from bank teller to bank president and sole owner, something possible in the early 1900s. He made loans to farmers and the townspeople of Garnett, and as her grandmother told her, a handshake from George W. Hunley was as good as a contract. The values of his time and his family ethics dictated that a man's honor was more important than any profit.

As Linnea watched the house slowly rising, with a rare afternoon to sit and talk to her friend, she decided to tell Sarah some of her family heritage story.

"Thinking about Everett and his risk taking reminds me of a relative. I had a great-great-grandfather, who at the age of sixteen drove a covered wagon from Crane Creek near Havana, Illinois, all the way to Kansas, to Garnett."

"I remember your mother saying something but I don't recall the details." Sarah thought about the mystery of her own family past, a heritage she wished she knew better.

"Well, Mom and Grandmother told me George Hunley took all the worldly possessions of his family by covered wagon, sometime in the eighteen seventies, while his mother and younger brother took the train. My mom still has the trunk where breakables were packed and transported. George's father had fought in the Civil War, on the side wanting to end slavery. When his father was a young man he left Kentucky because it was not against slavery. Because of his convictions, he went to Illinois, an anti-slavery state. After fighting in the Civil War he returned home to his family and their cabin at Crane Creek, near Havana, in central Illinois, but like many soldiers he eventually died from infection," Linnea explained.

"What a sad time in history. So many paid the price of slavery. I've often wondered, what if the founding fathers had never allowed slavery to start in this country? There never would have been the Civil War or the need for the Underground Railroad," said Sarah.

"It was a huge mistake to let slavery in, but seeing that it did happen, I'm glad there was an Underground Railroad. Didn't you tell me that Leroy and Binnie said black and white people worked together on the Underground Railroad, and that there was more cooperation between the races during that time than even today?" asked Linnea.

"I did tell you that. It's a shame there isn't more cooperation between people now," said Sarah.

"That's another reason why I'm passionate about saving this old house, besides needing a home! It represents a time when Americans, black and white, worked together to end slavery. And we know from Mrs. Wolter that this quaint house was part of the Underground Railroad, with the diary to prove it. Plus this house goes all the way back, before Civil War days, and not many houses are left in Havener from that era," said Linnea.

"When I receive the diary you know I'll share it. This is an important house to save, though I think just about any old house can be renovated and be useful." Sarah paused, watching the house inch up ever so slowly, and then asked, "Any more to your family story?"

"Well, as I was told it, George's mother, Ann Neville, my great-great-great-grandmother, sat in a rocking chair on the porch of their Illinois cabin at Crane Creek after her husband died. My mom told me Ann Neville sang her mournful songs as the whippoorwills called out, at least that's what my mother's mother told her. I can understand some of what my great-great-great grandmother must have felt, losing someone she loved too soon," Linnea reflected.

"I'm sure you do. I felt the same with my Mom dying when she was too young," Sarah told her.

"It must have been hard on you. I never heard you talk about it much," Linnea said, looking at her friend.

"You don't talk much either about Ray," said Sarah, not wanting to think about her mother now.

"It's too hard," Linnea said quietly. "I would rather focus on the house move and the future. My great-great-great-grandmother coped by packing up…with her two sons and her parents they all moved to Garnett, Kansas. She must have wanted to start over."

"Must have," Sarah confirmed.

Both women sat in silence as the house kept rising

slowly inch by inch. It would move and then stop moving and then start again after the workers made adjustments. The team was constantly assessing every shifting inch carefully. As Sarah sat watching the house rise up and halt and then rise again, she reflected upon her own history. She thought about her attempts at starting life over and about her own childhood grief, knowing how it was difficult at times to grieve.

She thought about how Linnea's great-great-great grandmother from three generations ago seemed to know a better way to mourn: in nature, with her family, and with the aid of song. She was able to express her grief over the loss of her husband as well as grieve the losses for her nation because of slavery and war. Sarah thought about how many had paid the price, reading that more than six hundred thousand people died as a result of that war. She wondered again what America would have been like if in its beginning slavery had never existed. She considered how different the evolution of a nation might have been, knowing the price of war with all its grief would not have been necessary had America not known the injustices of slavery.

Sarah had known more than her own share of grief and loss. Although it did not compare to the wounds of slavery or war, Sarah knew sorrow could never be measured for the one grieving. Grief knows no bounds in time nor measure, she told herself. Grief is painful, whatever the cause, be it her own pain, Linnea's suffering, or the grief of a relative from a century past.

As Sarah sat in silence, with the fate of the Underground Railroad house being determined, she reflected on the unusual coincidence that Linnea had the early loss of a husband, as did her great-great-great-grandmother. Both women over the centuries knew loss and sorrow. But for Linnea the lost knowledge of how to grieve, to genuinely mourn, was an additional loss.

This lost inheritance was evident not just for Linnea but in the American culture, as many people had lost their ability to grieve and mourn.

What Linnea did inherit from her relatives was an ability to take risks and to be resilient. As Linnea stood observing Everett and the crew working on her house she remembered more of her family story but decided not to talk about it now. Silently, as Linnea and Sarah watched her house moving in increments, she thought of her great-great-grandfather, the risk-taker who drove the covered wagon and who had his bank closed down in Garnett, Kansas, during the Depression. He was able to pay out to everyone what money was owed them, and he believed he could keep his bank going. But a government agency came in and closed him down. His response was to read while sitting on the second floor veranda in his beautiful, large old home, once built by an English immigrant but now torn down. There he proceeded to read all the works of William Shakespeare and many of the Greek philosophers, and afterwards he passed away from heart failure.

His huge home continued on for many years but Linnea knew it was torn down to make way for the "development" of the period starting in the late sixties. It was a fact that had always bothered Linnea because the loss of that house meant a certain loss of her family history. She remembered her mother telling her that a neighbor near the stately home said it was like losing an old friend to see the house get torn down. Linnea understood that many people had strong connections to old houses and their history, as was she developing her own link.

Growing up hearing this story and many others about her relatives helped Linnea better understand herself and her desire to save and move a house. She thought saving her old house from being torn down was in some way replacing what was lost to her family heritage when the large house was replaced by a smaller brick box of a building. She understood her perseverance and risk-taking were connected to those greats and great-greats who passed before her. Her great-great-grandfather's resilience had lived on in her, with her perseverance of moving the house. His mother's tenacity stayed alive in Linnea, just as she was certain the strength and resolve of enslaved families was passed down through the generations. She knew what it meant to be persistent, and it gave her a sense of respect for what families went through when they took the risk to run for their freedom.

She could not know what those risks must have been like, to have to run for freedom, but she knew she shared a certain persistence. She knew she had to have incredible perseverance to make her house move happen. Here she stood, before a house that had seen the cooperation of families resisting slavery and that had been a refuge for many. This was a house with an important history that otherwise would have been torn down had she not taken a risk. She understood how the values and abilities of her relatives that went before her, of their integrity and their perseverance, had survived in her.

Linnea also saw the same values and abilities surviving in those around her: in Sarah, in Linnea's parents, and in her new friend and house mover, Everett. Yes, he was a man of his word and was concerned about the people who saved houses. Everett knew he was helping people to have a home and this was more of a motivation to him than it was to make a profit. It was true he made money, as house moving had its cost as did the overhead wires have their fees. But it cost less than Linnea or Sarah imagined, and it was much less than building new.

Mother Nature was given a hand as well because a whole house was not thrown away. Sarah had a discussion with Everett about environmental issues and she raised a good point, he said, when she asked how much energy it takes to build new — not just in materials but in the transportation of them and all the other hidden costs. He said someone ought to do a study to calculate the real costs of building new. He also told her she would not be adding to the nationwide dumping of many old, structurally well built homes. Saving a house rather than tearing it down, they both had agreed, was the ultimate recycling project.

The women had been quiet for some time when Sarah decided to tell Linnea some of her new research about forests.

"Remember how concerned I felt about cutting down some of our trees for this house move onto new land?" Sarah asked as they watched the slow-going work of raising the house off the foundation. "Well, I have been reading and researching. You won't believe how many old growth forests have been cut down in the United States."

"I'll believe it. How many?" asked Linnea, as she observed Everett and crew focusing on the task at hand.

"They say it's more than ninety percent! How could we do this to our old forests," Sarah asked her friend, adding, "Today in Sweden, more than half of their country is made up of forests, and Japan has protected many of its forests."

"Then we have cut down too much here," Linnea said, shaking her head with sadness. "And some of these old growth forests take centuries to grow back — if they ever do. I'm sure it's a huge environmental problem."

"That's why people are trying to save trees now — because we've lost so many old forests," Sarah informed her. "I have been reading about the Tongass National Forest in southern Alaska. It's hard to believe it's rainforest, but they say it's one of the richest ecosystems anywhere—including tropical jungles!"

"I've never heard about it," Linnea admitted, not surprised by her friend's prolific reading.

"I read the Tongass makes up one-third of all old growth rainforests that are temperate. For the entire world," Sarah said.

"No kidding?" answered Linnea.

"And they still want to go in and cut down more trees. Some of those giant Sitka spruce trees are seven hundred years old! Already ninety percent of the giants among trees are gone. Those trees are more than ten feet in diameter and some are two hundred twenty-five feet tall! That is one big tree," Sarah said with awe.

"Somebody should start a movement," Linnea suggested. "'Save the Sitka Trees.' I have never even heard about giant Sitka spruce trees. I'll write a newspaper article about them. Why didn't you tell me about this before?"

"I'm still learning about those amazing trees," Sarah told her. "I'm also researching western hemlock and cedar. And honestly, I still don't know how to deal with my feelings about ninety percent of Alaksa's big trees having been cut down already, along with most of the old growth forests in America. I find it very upsetting."

"It's an incredible loss," Linnea agreed, feeling overwhelmed herself.

"And besides, you did not tell me about your house moving idea either when you first knew about it," Sarah reminded her, knowing they were both surprised by what seemed like secrets for the first time in their friendship.

"At least we are saving the trees in this old house," Linnea commented. "That is some consolation." She paused, then added, "Hey, I bet the trees in this house are from old growth forests."

"I bet you're right! Let's ask Everett when he takes a break," Sarah suggested, as both women sat quietly once again, watching the house preparation and reflecting on their land of birth and its losses.

As Sarah sat quietly, she thought about how house movers appreciate old houses and their natural resources. They know their value. Everett had once told her he had never seen a house that was not fixed up after it was moved. "No, I have never seen one that was not improved. There is a pride of ownership when you save an old house," he told her. Sarah wondered if it was because the task of planning a house move was so consuming that the owner feels all the more linked to the house they saved and moved. It was a healthy sense of roots for an immigrant, wandering people, to a land of many dreams.

Sarah felt as if the Underground Railroad house had called out to them, asking to be saved. It was calling for them to honor its history and resources, as well as all those who lived before and walked the halls of the old house. It was calling for a respect of the history of the Underground Railroad where both black and white people worked together in the name of a higher purpose.

The house defied destruction, just as black women and black men defied slavery, and white men and white women fought against slavery. They all defied being objectified, defied the inhumanity of slavery. This house, this strong house, continued in its own way a history of defiance in not being torn down. Yes, the meaningful history of the fight to end human slavery wanted to be kept alive with a house that called to a people in the new millennium to remember and learn from the past about injustice.

So the house did rise, just as a people held down did rise up to a greater humanity, and would keep rising. The house, with a rich story to tell, was lifted by the intentions of a man and two women who cared about history and nature. Everett continued the momentum of the Underground Railroad as his equipment slowly lifted the house a good foot up, keeping it level and supported. Then he built more cribbing with wooden railroad ties, square columns with one row of railroad ties crisscrossed over another until they reached close to the bottom of the wheels attached to the beams supporting the house.

Once all the wooden ties were stacked, almost filling half of the basement, the same metal strips used for airplane landings similar to the other house moves the women had witnessed, were placed on top of the planks on the wood piers. Those runners on the wood planks on the cribbing provided the support for the wheels under the house. It was those simple metal strips and small wheels on which the historical house would gingerly move. So this is how the house would roll off the empty space of the basement, Sarah thought as she stood in awe. Once again the house moved, rolling slowly but steadily off the foundation and on to solid ground. Linnea stood next to Sarah and then looked at her with a small grin.

"Now you see how it's done. How amazing is that house on wheels," she stated.

"You know it," agreed Sarah.

"Hey, Linnea," said one of the crew, trying to tease her, "you better hope no one comes in the night and hitches up the old house and wheels her away."

Everett noticed her surprised and concerned look.

"Knock it off, you guys," he said. "You know that has never happened. Besides, who would have a truck powerful enough, you wise crackers."

The laughter faded, and Linnea felt reassured. She was content with her three days spent with Sarah, watching her house rising above ground, in awe of the process it took to raise the house.

"Everybody loves a house move," said Linnea.

"So it seems," said a wise Everett.

At that, both women said their goodbyes to Everett and the crew, thanking them for a job well done. They left with excited anticipation of the day to come: the day the old 1853 Underground Railroad house would be on the move.

15

House Moving Day

Blair and Julia were excited to be out of school so they could watch the house move down the street. It was early morning as they sat drawing at Sarah's kitchen table. They made colorful pictures of houses on wheels, part of the "series" they had been creating for weeks. The wheel size varied, the colors of the house changed dramatically, but the theme was always the same: houses on the move. The girls had unicorns pulling orange houses, dragons pushing lime green and yellow houses, trolls hiding under the wheels of a house, and lavender angels surrounding golden boxes deemed home sweet home on wheels. Their artwork was a helpful outlet for them while their mothers were busy with the details of getting ready for house moving day.

Everyone was up early with plans to meet at Linnea's parents' home for breakfast and then to go together to see the house move. Linnea had already been to her old house once that morning to check that all was going as planned. The rain that had threatened luckily moved north, so placed before them was a beautiful Midwestern day, with a sky packed full of white puff clouds like puzzle pieces set in soft blue. Good weather made it easier for the move, and it meant a bigger crowd would gather to watch.

Everyone was on board, except Tyler, who was adamant about not going. Sarah was so disappointed and far more hurt than he would have wanted to know. Even if Tyler at first resented Linnea getting the house, Sarah thought he should be over it by now. She knew he would have found the house move fascinating and would have enjoyed being a part of the whole process. But there was no talking to Tyler. His mind was set on his way of seeing things, even if it was a distorted view. Sarah was left without her partner to share in her excitement and a familiar loneliness was with her, one that stirred her childhood history.

Sarah was determined to not let it spoil her day or Julia's. Even though Tyler had argued with her about Julia missing school, he knew he was on shaky ground, so he finally dropped it. One area Sarah would always hold her own was with matters concerning their daughter, and Sarah had continually made good choices regarding Julia. She was a terrific mother; Tyler would never dispute that fact — even if he forgot to tell her she was doing a great job.

After everyone had a hot breakfast of thick, French toast made with cinnamon and fresh cream prepared by Linnea's mother, Kathy, they all piled into vehicles to drive to town. Her mother could always be counted on to give to family and friends. She was often a behind-the-scenes person who was sometimes taken for granted, but today her work was given its due praise.

There was energy in the air, a fresh excitement as if that rainstorm had actually passed through and renewed the atmosphere. There had not been a house move in Havener, Illinois, for a number of years, and people were eagerly awaiting it as a highlight.

Linnea and Sarah knew the newspaper reporters would be there, with cameras and notepads in hand. One reporter was coming all the way from a big Chicago newspaper because Linnea's father had connections. When the reporter heard about the possible assignment, he had to fast talk his boss into letting him come down. His boss, Jim, had known Linnea's father when both men were fresh in the business. Jim agreed to send him more as a favor to Bill than for the story itself.

Jim sent Garret because he knew he would have the sensitivity needed for the story. He knew his warmth in his interviewing, which was never intrusive, had an uncanny way of getting people to open up and share their life stories. Garret had made the trip several hours west of Chicago the day before and was up early and on the street. Like many others, he was looking forward to the house moving down Maple Avenue.

After Linnea and her extended family left the stone house and approached Havener, they could see people lining the streets in anticipation of watching the house move. It was a larger turnout than expected, but then a house on wheels moving down the street was an unusual sight to see. All the police were at strategic places and had closed off certain streets to traffic. The crews for electric, phone, and cable were all present, and it appeared the house move would go like clockwork. Linnea and family were able to get through road blocks and arrive at the old house site where Grace and Rollo Wolter stood watch. They had come back from Florida just for the house move and were happy to be visiting and staying with friends.

"Hi, Mr. and Mrs. Wolter," said Linnea.

"Well, hello there, house moving lady," said Rollo. "We're sure glad you saved our humble abode."

"You certainly have a beautiful day for a house move," said Grace wistfully.

"We do have a lovely day," said Sarah, hugging her gently.

"Thank you again for giving us the house," Linnea said. "I still can't quite believe it's all happening today."

"Well, it's a near perfect day for it. And we are just so glad you and Blair can find our home to be of use," said Mr. Wolter, relieved the house would not be torn down.

Everyone else said their greetings and chatted, the small talk of the Midwest evident while they waited for the action to begin, seeing a near-thirty-ton historic Underground Railroad house move down the road. The house was scheduled to pull out at nine A.M. In some states, Linnea had learned that houses can only be moved at night in the wee small hours so traffic is undisturbed. But Linnea's house had the advantage of light, the fun of a curious crowd, and the chance to be newsworthy. It promised to be an eventful day.

Leroy and Binnie then joined the crowd with Linnea and Sarah and other friends. Sarah was pleased they had made it to the house move, and she walked over to greet them.

"Leroy, Binnie, can you believe it's happening today?" she asked them.

"You know we thought you could pull this off, Sarah. What a sight to see. That house is part of my heritage, my people's history, so I would not miss this day," Leroy reminded her.

"That house is part of all our history," said Binnie. "It's good to respect what courage people had back then."

"And what courage these two women have today to move this house," added Leroy.

The two women friends were being rewarded by this day of moving and its promised accomplishment. Both women had earned this remarkable day, and the old historic house gifted to Linnea would soon meet its fate. They felt excitement and anxiety mixed with a rush of adrenalin. It was the feeling of preliminary joy and the promise of relief for a well-planned house move.

Since it had been some years that anyone cared enough to save an old house, everyone was interested. Many other moves had made history before this one, all over the United States be it Wisconsin, Nevada, or North Carolina and all over Canada. For two centuries industrious and frugal Americans and Canadians worked at saving and moving their homes. It was part of the entrepreneurial spirit ingrained in the culture and of an immigrant people who knew how to meet big challenges. Everett exemplified just such a spirit. Like most Americans he descended from immigrants who had come searching for a new way of life. He followed a long line of people with a unique way of thinking, just like Sarah's father who had traveled halfway around the world to immigrate and create a new life. And Sarah had continued the same search in her own unique way.

Sarah was the observer, always taking in. She did the same with the house moving project, watching and learning. As she stood waiting for the move she recalled hearing Everett say, "No two houses are alike." Sarah thought it's just like the uniqueness of people: no two are alike, and yet they are so similar in their humanity. Everett had added, "That's what keeps me working on them. No two houses are alike and every single time she's a new challenge."

Everett had enjoyed working on Linnea's house moving project, both in planning with the women, whom he thought were a good team, and in lifting the house. "She" had her challenges but all had gone quite smoothly. He could sense when a house was just "meant to be" for someone. He knew it because each day had a flow and the preparation went smoothly. He knew Linnea's hard work and planning were part of it, but he knew there was an ease in a project when a house and an owner were well matched.

Those past weeks he had thought about Sarah, who he could tell wanted — needed — a house. He reflected on how people did not so much deserve a house but had the need of one. He knew everyone needs a home and it kept him moving houses. He told her that sometimes a house just has a way of coming to a person. One day he told her, "Look for the signs. Watch for the signs and the right house will come your way. I've seen it happen."

Sarah understood "signs", like seeing a bird fly above at a sacred moment in time and the synchronism of such timing makes an underlying unity apparent. Sometimes a "sign" might lead to a challenge set before her, one that was more of a test than an obstacle. Yes, Sarah knew signs. She even had sensed a few times, hints from the universe that the old Underground Railroad house had called out to her. But then she assumed it was to help save it, not to live in it. Or rather to be a visitor in the house, as Sarah had been, in Linnea's house and other homes. She always was a visitor. This led her to say to others more than once her views about humanity. "We are all just visitors upon this planet," she would tell them.

Everett privately hoped he could help move a house for Sarah. He knew people, and he knew Sarah had some deep need that a good house could heal. Her homeless past was an unknown to him, but he knew on some level she had an unmet need for a place to call home. He knew it from his keen perceptiveness. He was that good of a house mover.

The house was finally ready. Everett, who was not one for the limelight, was center stage as he directed the crew for his current house move. He wore a red T-shirt and blue jeans and he kept everything under control. The house had been hitched to the truck that only he would drive, no one else. The latch to the truck was secure, but appeared small in contrast to what it must pull.

"We are ready to go!" Everett said, as he jumped in his truck hitched to the house.

"The tire blocks are moved. Pull out!" shouted Everett's son, Tom. He was another skilled house mover who had learned his trade from his father and grandfather.

"All clear," said another worker, Kevin.

With all eyes on the house, Everett carefully pulled out, hauling the tons of weight on the steel beams with attached wheels that guided the load of the house. There were a few shouts from crew members but all was starting out slowly and smoothly as Linnea's house was pulled out onto the road.

The house proceeded down the first stretch. It was a terrific sight to see: what's almost always stable and sedentary—a house rooted to the earth—to be on the move. The sounds were unique, both in the hush of the crowd and the soft moans from the old 1853 house as its heavy weight gently moved forward. On occasion there was spontaneous clapping as the house entered a new block of viewers, as if this move was theater in the making—like Midwest conceptual art—with a house moving past old, graceful trees on a blissful early summer day.

Linnea and her daughter Blair were behind the house as it moved. They were walking together, with Julia next to Blair. Sarah walked behind them along with Linnea's mother and father, her former guardians. Both women felt similar feelings, like shouting from the rooftops.

"Sarah, we did it! All that planning and now it's moving!" said Linnea.

"Who knew we could ever get a house moved?" Sarah added, "But we did it!"

"It took patience and perseverance, you two," said Bill. "Congratulations!"

Sarah could imagine herself with Linnea joyously shouting on the roof of the very house as it moved down the street. Linnea felt the sheer joy of the moving house, mixed with anticipation for the celebration to come that evening, with a reservation shadowed by doubts about everything going as planned.

As the 1853 house progressed down the next streets, workers were everywhere lifting phone lines, or covering with steel plates different lines dropped to the ground, always coordinating together, ever watchful so nothing would go wrong. A crowd of friends joined the family behind the house to walk with the old home on its route to a new paradise. It was a parade of sorts, a ceremonial procession where the weight of all prior wounds, all injuries to the soul were lifted, just as the old house was raised and carried, as a result of the care and generosity of many.

"How long will it take to get to Oak Street?" asked Bill.

"It's a mile and a half with an estimated time of travel of less than one hour," said Linnea.

"You have it all under control don't you, honey," said her father. He was impressed by her organizational skills, which he had seen before at their newspaper.

"Yes, as much as I can. It's up to Everett now. Isn't it amazing to see it actually go down the street, after all the planning? It's thrilling!" Linnea exclaimed.

"Linnea, can you believe this is actually happening?" asked Sarah with excitement.

"No, I can't believe this day is finally here, and we're walking behind my new house, on wheels!" said Linnea happily.

The 1853 house journeyed past old, tall trees and a few oaks that were even older than the house. The house passed other homes old and new, markers of time from generations past and present. Garret from Chicago took pictures during every phase of the move. He was a discreet yet important presence, keeping record of a unique house on the move. As Garret did his work, Everett and crew did theirs while other crews completed their duties with skill and focus.

The house kept its movement sustained as if it had a presence of its own accord: the stately presence of a house on an almost silent journey. Now it seemed a new pride was visible, surrounding the house as it continued its journey, as if the frame and walls appeared slightly taller with new dignity. Gracefully the home moved down the street, a solitary house with a remarkable history. It was helped with the well wishes of observers who projected onto the house their pleasure in seeing the old, Underground Railroad house saved and on the move.

Leroy was pleased to see the house moving down the road. No one understood just how meaningful it felt to him in saving the 1853 house that was part of his people's history. It was hard to put into words for him for the moment. When he caught up with Linnea and Sarah, he tried to express some of how he felt.

"You ladies have done an outstanding job planning all this. It means a good deal to me that you are saving this house," said Leroy.

"I'm glad we can save it, and thank you for the compliment," Linnea said. "You know, Sarah was a huge part of making this happen."

"Yes, but none of this could have happened without Everett!" Sarah added.

"He's our man, yes indeed. The man of the hour," added Leroy. "I am so glad you all did this. It's good for history, and for our town, that the old Underground Railroad place has been saved," he stated, as he observed the house on the move.

Who would have guessed an old house could be worth so much to so many? The old home had been a safe house for people seeking shelter from the injustice of slavery, and again the house had become a harbor of hope. Once a haven for freedom seekers, now the house would become a haven for Linnea and her daughter. For Sarah, it had become a symbol of hope for her future because she was able to perceive it as such, unlike Tyler whose perception was far different. For the Wolters, the home's surviving meant part of their family history would continue. It also meant the house would be a monument of America's troubled past and transcendent history of the Underground Railroad.

The house moved forward. People walked the journey while making history on a small, sacred road to a destination not fully understood. The house, regal in its standing, pressed on with the help of a multitude of workers. The stoplight that was overhanging at the corner was swung out for the house to make the corner with ease, and then swung back after the house turned and headed north to its final resting place. Heading north as did many slaves journey for the hope of freedom. It was north to an unknown future, but one worthy of the risk.

There was a gentle incline as the house approached the near tree-filled land where it would meet its fate. But with the skills of the movers and the prepared road on Linnea's property, the old house finally came to a pause while those involved stopped to talk. Everett got out of his truck.

"We are gonna leave her parked here for today Linnea, and return back tomorrow to set her into the foundation hole. We will do some of the prep work today and then finish up tomorrow. She's secure on your land," Everett said.

"I remember you said the house move and some preparation would be enough for today. As you know, the excavator has the foundation hole filled with three feet of stone, so whenever you are ready," said Linnea.

"We'll place some railroad ties in the foundation hole today and be back with more ties early in the morning and set to work. It won't take us too long to finish building up the ties for the cribbing under the house. We will go up a good twelve feet so she can stand ready for the foundation workers to start the nine-foot basement walls. Don't worry about the old house. She'll be fine," said her house mover.

Sarah, along with Bill and Kathy, Blair and Julia, Leroy and Binnie, and Grace and Rolla stood watching as Linnea handled the details. Other friends and Garret, the reporter, stood nearby, the click of the camera heard occasionally while easy house negotiations ensued. Then Sarah watched as Linnea turned to everyone, smiling.

"We did it! This old eighteen-fifty-three house is saved!" shouted Linnea.

People cheered and clapped. Everyone was joyful that the house move had gone smoothly. Everett, house mover extraordinaire, was given a full round of applause. Sarah and Linnea hugged one another and then hugged the girls, while hearty handshakes were the order of the day for many people. Everyone felt the unusual happiness and fulfillment that comes only from a house move. As things began winding down, a few curious people investigated near the hole dug out where the house would sit on the cribbing of wooden railroad ties, soon to be resting high in the air until the basement walls would be ready for the house to sit for another 150 years. Other people walked by the trees and talked about the day, their perceptions, and reflected upon their own homes. Still others discussed the importance of saving the historical Underground Railroad house, even if it had to be moved from its original site. As the excitement for the day was over, the crowd started to disperse, taking with them the joy of watching the house move of a unique home.

16

Celebrations

Everyone present was enjoying the gathering to help celebrate the successful move of Linnea and Blair's new home. Little lights strung outside surrounded the guests like starlight created by human will. Linnea's parents' home offered itself to the visitors who moved freely in and out of the old quarry stone house, with walls more solid than anyone understood. They were strong walls that exemplified the courage of Linnea's family during their trials over the years, and of the human striving by known and unknown families that had once lived in the stone cottage.

Many women, and the men who liked to cook, had prepared their favorite foods to share, so a good display of a Midwest potluck was abundantly spread out on flowered tablecloths. Like small, colorful offerings to the gods of house moving, foods were given freely so to nourish the good that was growing in a community celebrating itself.

Friends played music with sounds following the breeze of the soft night air. There were a number of musicians who had been taught by Linnea's mother, a music teacher who could always draw in a group willing to blend their various instruments. Tonight was unique because harp and dulcimer were added to the usual classical guitar and piano. Someone even arrived with a cello and then an oboe, and so strings were plucked and notes flew into the dark for an evening of music with specific flair. The sounds called to the souls of listeners, hinting at what Sarah whispered to her good friend, Linnea: "We are of this world and we are not of this world."

Those closely involved with the house move and even those on the outer circumference who were supportive felt the need for this celebration. Even Everett arrived, although he had never known someone to have a party on the evening of the same day the house had moved. He rarely went to parties and Linnea, who was glad he had arrived, had to twist his arm to get him to make the drive. He did it out of respect for her past loss and her sorrow.

The evening air was pristine. It was one of those rare but perfect nights—cool enough to be invigorating but not enough to chill. Visible stars appeared especially vibrant, far away from town lights, and the dark swallowed up any left over tensions of the day. The soft moon was glowing a muted crimson just above the horizon as if mimicking the sun, teasing out its reflection. Sarah thought it a mystery that such a celestial body as the moon existed, full of reflective light. That unusual moonlight seemed to deliver the sunlight softly, in an intimate way, as its light played with the wind in the trees surrounding the stone house. The leaves rustled like background sound for the music while the soft breeze nestled the friends who were good enough to come and help celebrate.

The bluff's edge had been buffered with tables set up and a makeshift fence so everyone was safely contained while enjoying the evening out of doors. Most of the guests had arrived, including Binnie and Leroy.

As retired farmers still living on their land in their old farm house, it was rare they went out, but this day had been an exception, along with the evening. And as one of the few inter-racial couples in the area, and having faced the ignorance of racism in their younger years, they continued their tendency to keep to themselves. But tonight was different as they had never gone to a party honoring the move of an Underground Railroad house. Linnea knew Sarah would be happy knowing the couple had come not only to the house move but also this evening to help them celebrate.

Earlier that day, while the house moved down the streets, Linnea had seen Garret. She told him he was invited to the celebration, noticing him now when he arrived. She wondered how he had been given his name, Garret, an uncommon first name, and she assumed it had a story. She also wondered what he thought about her house moving story. She felt fabulous about the day, even if at first she was somewhat tense. Yet the more her house moved down the road, the more certain she felt that she had taken the right course. Her perseverance, she told herself, and her courage, were really paying off.

Garret had noticed Linnea as well when he came in the door and wanted to tell her what a pleasure it had been to share in her house move and to thank her for inviting him to her evening party. Feeling an unaccustomed shyness without understanding why, he walked over to see her. He also wanted to ask some questions he had about the house move for the article he was writing.

"Hello, Linnea, we met briefly, earlier today. I'm Garret," he said, giving her a solid Midwest handshake.

"Yes, hello." She shook his hand in response, wondering when in the 1800s did women and men start shaking hands. "Sorry I could not talk much earlier today, but it was a bit hectic," said Linnea.

"I understand. It's not everyday you move a house," Garret said. He noticed Sarah close by, watching them and making eye contact with Linnea as if they had some link beyond words.

"To be honest, I'm relieved it's over. But what a day. It's one I will never forget." she said. "By the way, do you mind if I ask you about your first name, Garret?"

"Not at all. I was given the name after my grandfather, Garret Louis Stone. He wasn't a reporter, but he was in printing and he knew a lot about how books are made. I knew him well, but I wish I could have spent more time with him," he explained.

He found himself observing Linnea's face, liking her strong profile and the softness in her brown eyes that made him feel tender and sorrowful for her loss. He had learned from his boss in Chicago about her husband's death. Garret had known he was sent because his boss felt he would be sensitive to her story, and he found himself wondering how she coped with her loss. Not the usual question, but Garret was a man much like his grandfather, who gently liked to get to the truth of a matter. To gain an understanding, and thus to expand his world, were primary goals for Garret, and to do it with curiosity and empathy—and without judgment. His was a search for truth. These traits made him good at his job and important in the newspaper world. He was respected by those who knew the value of such an approach, one he took not just to work but in how he lived his life.

"My grandfather, Garret Stone, had wanted to break into newspaper reporting just after World War II. He tried at the same newspaper where I now work, and he knew he was close to getting hired. But the job was not offered to him, so he kept his job as a delivery trucker for a printing company. He was able to work up into management; those were the days when you could do that. My grandfather told me more than once that his life would have been quite different if he had been offered that newspaper job," he said.

So the younger Garret was the fulfillment of the creative drive unmet in his grandfather, he told her. Garret went on to tell Linnea about a story his grandfather had written about sailors returning from World War II and how well it was written. He told her how his style had influenced his own, but didn't think to tell her how his grandfather's values made the difference in how he worked as a reporter.

"My family has stories passed down. I'm glad to know the family history," he said.

Garret then asked Linnea about the house, how she found out about it, its history on the Underground Railroad, and about the land to where it had just been moved. He kept a mental record of all her information, trusting it to his keen memory, knowing he would momentarily write it down. He asked if he could meet with her tomorrow at the new house site, and they agreed on a time.

As Linnea spoke she also found herself talking about her family history. As she verbalized her links with the past she became aware of a heritage, a timeline of her family which joined with her own individual timeline. She had a sense of how both she and Garret shared a respect for their past relatives.

There was ease and pleasure in their conversing and both noticed it. Linnea felt inspired and open, and enjoyed discussing ideas with him. It had been a long while since she had allowed herself to be this free with a man. She assumed she could let her guard down now because her house had made it safely to its destination.

While Linnea talked with Garret, Sarah was talking with Binnie and Leroy. She loved their company, soaked it up because they were two of the wisest and most introspective people she knew. They had been involved in the Civil Rights movement and over time had told Sarah stories about the risks, traumas, and successes of those days past. Sarah had listened intently to gain a better understanding of America and its complex history. Tonight's conversation though focused on an earlier time in history.

"After we heard about you moving the house we read as much as we could find about the Underground Railroad. We found a lot of interesting things on the Internet. The reference librarians have also been very helpful at our local library. We especially enjoyed a book called *The Underground Railroad in Illinois,* and even corresponded with the author via email. I am sure our local librarians will help you get the book and other reading materials from other libraries. That is, once you recover from helping Linnea move the house," Binnie said.

"Actually, Grace Wolter told me about the same book. I look forward to getting it," said Sarah.

Leroy gave her a steady look and said, "So much of the Underground Railroad is hard to document because it was not safe to keep records. We have to piece together that courageous part of American history."

"I've read about Harriet Tubman and Sojourner Truth. They are heroines in my eyes. I especially liked reading Sojourner's words…that passage, 'And Ain't I a Woman?' She was quite the orator," said Sarah.

"She was quite the speaker, and for a woman of her day, she was ahead of her time," agreed Binnie, adding, "Harriet Tubman was my favorite heroine when I learned about her in the sixth grade. Of all that I learned in school, reading a book about her stands out the most.

I think I was hungry for stories about daring women, ones who took a stand for justice."

"It was not that long ago, when you think of the time span of history, that she lived and struggled to end slavery. Slavery existed far too long in our human history, for thousands of years. The fight in our country to end it I think made a world contribution, even if slavery never should have been brought to America in the first place. We have to keep the houses like Linnea's, that we know were stopping places, depots they called them, on the Underground Railroad, as part of the puzzle of America's history," said Leroy.

"Her house is one of those parts of the puzzle," commented Sarah. She thought about her own life and all the missing puzzle pieces.

"And you helped save it from being torn down." Leroy smiled at Sarah and said, "We all know it's better if a historic house is not moved, but there was no choice with this house. No choice. That was quite a show today with that big, old house going down the street. Now it's saved from demolition."

"We're glad—for many reasons. We hope it will help Linnea and Blair," said Binnie.

"I'm sure it will," Sarah answered. Seeing another guest arriving, she excused herself to go and meet them. While she was walking through the crowd Everett spoke to her from behind.

"Sarah. How about that house move?" he remarked.

"Our hats are off to you, Sir Everett. I can't imagine how you do it, over and over, how you move house after house," she said.

"Each one is a challenge." He was a man of few words. "We have to get a house for you now. I'll move it for you," Everett offered.

"I guess we do," Sarah said, feeling shy. She was glad she had other guests to greet and walked to meet them.

Her embarrassment made him think she didn't feel as worthy as those who owned homes. Everett knew about people from all his years of dealing with them and their house moves. He was again aware of a need in Sarah for a home, and that she needed help to get a house. This house for a dollar was not the first house that would help a family. He promised himself he would watch for a place that might come his way that could work for Sarah and her family.

Sarah greeted a few more guests and then walked back to talk with Leroy, who was standing with Bill. She felt the comfort of being with people who knew her well and valued what she had to contribute. Tonight she needed such solace. She had been feeling as if a part of her was drifting away, as if she did not fully belong, as if her body was present yet she was detached. She watched her surroundings with her attention partially removed from her experience. She did not understand whether it was because of her different heritage or her homeless past that she felt detached. She wondered if it was because of her ethereal longings, but often she felt as if she were only partially present in groups of people.

Leroy and Bill were discussing more about history, and their converstaion helped Sarah feel back in the present moment. Leroy didn't miss a beat as Sarah rejoined them.

"You know, Sarah, the Underground Railroad was the first, large-scale civil disobedience movement in America at that time. And it was an integrated movement, where people overcame prejudice and worked together. This is why it is important, and because it led to the Civil Rights movement," Leroy told her.

"So the Underground Railroad was for the most part another nonviolent movement, like in India with Gandhi, leading their nonviolent freedom movement," Sarah responded.

"Well, I never made that connection," Leroy said to her, smiling at her ability to find historical links.

"And I never knew the Underground Railroad movement led to the Civil Rights movement," Sarah said, smiling back at him.

"It did, rightly so," Leroy told her, pausing before he asked, "Do you know about the writer, Harriet Ann Jacobs?"

"I'm afraid I don't, but I can tell I am just about to learn more history from you," she said with humor.

"Yes, you are, child. If you want to understand why people were passionately opposed to slavery, read her book. She wrote one of the few slave narratives, as they call them, written by a woman. Now, she published in 1861. It is a chilling autobiography of the terrible crimes of slavery and yet still this woman found her way to freedom. She was one woman of integrity. Read her book and you will see," said Leroy, adding, "She changed her name for publishing to Linda Brent. She was afraid of harm coming to her family because she wrote the honest truth."

"She was ahead of her time," said Binnie, rejoining their conversation. "She was hoping her book could help women still trapped in slavery, and help all people who were not free. She completed her autobiography in 1859 but it took until 1861, after the Civil War started, to publish it, and she never got her due recognition back then."

"It's a remarkable story. She hid for almost seven years in a small attic space and through a small hole she watched her children, even though they did not know she was hiding close by 'em. She finally escaped and was later reunited with her two children," Leroy said, shaking his head in remembrance of this woman's difficult life.

"I will read her book. I want to better understand why people were passionate about helping people escape to freedom—and how the injustice of slavery motivated people," Sarah told them.

"Injustice is a word that does not tell the sorrows of slavery. Families being torn apart, people tortured physically and in the mind. There was no worse time for my people in American history," said Leroy. "No. Injustice does not cover what people suffered.

"I can see how important the Underground Railroad is, to remember the sacrifices people made," said Sarah, adding, "and to see a link to the Civil Rights era."

"And we made a few more of those connections ourselves, tonight, after the old Underground Railroad house was on the move," Leroy said, smiling at Sarah and thinking of the learning they had shared—and the adventure.

"We did, Leroy," she said.

Sarah excused herself to go and check on Julia and Blair. As she observed the girls playing, she found herself watching Everett and Linnea talking. Then she overheard Everett say he liked working with Linnea and Sarah and how the day had gone well. Linnea told Everett the pleasure was all hers in working with him and knowing she could count on him to handle her home with skill. Sarah knew she meant she was forever thankful for his caring efforts for the home full of the promise of new hope. Even more than thankful, Sarah knew Linnea was touched to her very soul for the chance to live in a wonderful home filled with a unique history and to be able start a new life.

Sarah appreciated her friend's gratitude, even if it was difficult for Linnea to put the depth of her feeling into words. She was genuinely glad for her friend's opportunity because altruism came easily to Sarah. Still, Sarah felt a strong longing for something greater than she had yet discovered in Havener, Illinois, and it was more than a desire for a house of her own.

While talking to Linnea, Everett noticed she looked different and not just because her house had been moved. Her complexion had a glow as if life was emanating from her. He knew why, as he was a wise and observant man. He knew when there was a connection between a man and a woman. He thought he had better check out this city man, Garret, to see if he was worthy of her.

While the adults pursued their conversations, Julia and Blair were having a grand old time on a star-lit school night. They ran in and out of the house, jiggled a few strands of sparkling lights and then were re-directed to the dress-up box. The girls were as entertaining as ever in their antics of dressing up in imaginary arrays of thrown together costumes. Many of the guests were enjoying the girl's creativity as it reminded them of days less demanding and full of playfulness.

After everyone had visited and eaten the delicious home cooked food, Everett came up to see Sarah and Linnea, reminding them he had a busy day ahead with setting the house up high in the foundation hole. The house would be put in place before the basement walls would be built and poured. This was because the walls of the house and the foundation had to match perfectly, and it was easier to plum down for wall placement when the house was in position. As Everett had told her, there was no worse problem than trying to match a house after resting it on a foundation that did not line up. Most house movers preferred to move the house into the hole, rest it on cribbing, and wait for the foundation to be poured and dried for ten days. Then they "dropped" the house on the new basement walls.

Linnea's house still had to be put up on cribbing before her foundation work could begin. Stacking up the wood of the support piers and setting the house down on them was a good half days work or more, he reminded Linnea, and he had to get home to rest. So Everett, the quiet man who took on challenge after challenge of moving houses, said goodbye to Linnea after she thanked him repeatedly, more than she needed from her house mover's perspective. Before he could exit she made an announcement to the guests.

"Before Everett leaves, I just want to thank him for a great house moving day!" she said as people applauded him. "I also want to thank Grace and Rolla for the incredible gift of their house, even though they could not be here tonight. Finally, I want to thank my dear friend, Sarah, for all her help and for all the sacrifices she made. Sarah, thank you!" Another round of clapping ensued.

After Everett left, other people began to say their goodbyes and leave for their homes. The sound of music had been quieter for some time, and now most of the varied instruments had phased out. Leroy and Binnie bid farewell to Sarah and Linnea and to Linnea's parents, with Binnie thanking Linnea's mother for providing such a nice celebration. Both women knew much of their work went unnoticed, as much of women's work did, but they knew how important it was to the fabric of their family and their community. Kathy then thanked the musicians for coming with instruments in hand. Everyone seemed to leave with a fulfillment that comes when true community is shared. After the last farewells with their guests, Linnea and Sarah hugged, with both women feeling a sense of accomplishment with the house move.

"Sarah, thank you again, for all your help with planning the house move. I could not have done it without you," said Linnea.

"Yes, you could have. You are one resilient woman. And you were great at organizing all the details. I just helped a bit," said Sarah.

"You know you did a lot of the work. It means so much to me that you helped. So when will I see you tomorrow?" asked Linnea.

"Nine A.M., I'll be there," said Sarah. At that both women said a final goodbye. Sarah gathered up her daughter, Julia, who was tired but still reluctant to leave, and they headed for home. Sarah had to again put to rest some of her own feelings of longing for a home and settle her thoughts about having to face a defiant husband, if he was home. It was easier to just be in the present moment than deal with so many thoughts and feelings. Being with her daughter always helped Sarah be in the here and now, as Julia was spontaneous and alive to the present, like most children.

Sarah started the conversation. "What did you think about the house move?"

"It was great, Mom. I wish I could have been inside the house when it moved down the road," said Julia.

"That would have been fun!" Sarah agreed.

"Blair and I could have waved from the widow, and you could have seen us," Julia fantasized. Like all children her age, she liked when her mother's attention was focused on her.

"I would have enjoyed waving back at you. I can just imagine you in the house. I did read about an elderly woman who stayed in her cabin while it was moved," Sarah told her daughter.

"That would have been so great. But it was still neat to see a whole house move down a street. I am glad we read that picture book, *The Town That Moved*. Where was that town?" Julia asked.

"Hibbing, Minnesota, and it's a true story. All those houses were moved, just like your Auntie Linnea's.

Today was quite a day, a day to remember," her mother added. They rode in silence, with Julia soon falling asleep and Sarah thinking about all that had happened that remarkable day and evening. As she drove toward her place she felt overwhelmed but happy with everything that had transpired. Then she focused on what the next day might bring, as the setting up of the old house on piers promised to be just as interesting, if different, as house raising and house moving day.

17

Thief in the Night

This is justice, Tyler style, he thought to himself. Added to his list of poor justifications was the thought: I'm right to do this because Sarah earned it in all she has suffered and in all the help she gave away to Linnea with her silly schemes. Tyler did not understand their bond of friendship nor did he grasp how love could be given so freely to a friend. Sarah said it was a mutual give and take, but to Tyler's eyes, it had been unequal from the start, when their so-called "poverty stricken" distant relative had been taken in. He figured the family had gotten enough credit for their good deed of helping Sarah.

He was bitter about Sarah's difficulties and now his own. Where was *their* dream house? That great American dream house had only stayed a dream, one less tangible to him than even to Sarah when she was a homeless child. It was his bitterness, anger, and determination to right a wrong that caused him to devise a plan. It was a plan that would undo them all, if it succeeded, a plan that was a poor answer to a prayer he never sent. It was a plot that as far as he knew had never been tried, a theft never attempted. He had worked out all the details, and he was ready to execute his plan of taking what he thought belonged to Sarah. He was prepared to steal the house for her.

He knew the local bar would be the watering hole for a certain crew member and so when Tyler walked in he was not surprised to see Rickie sitting down, nurturing a few. Tyler sat down next to him at the bar, just as he had the night before.

"Hey, I didn't see you at the house move today," remarked Rickie.

"I had to work, just like the rest of the poor fools, just like you," said Tyler. "Hey, let me buy a round of drinks for us."

"I could use a few. You missed a good house move. It was a piece of cake; everything went real smooth," Rickie said.

"So I heard," said Tyler, lying. He had not been home when Sarah and Julia had returned earlier that evening. He had intentionally stayed away, not wanting to see his wife.

Tyler kept the drinks coming, just enough to loosen Rickie up so he would do the unthinkable, but not so many he could not stand up. Tyler kept drinking his soft drinks, which he said were mixed, as he knew no one liked drinking alone, and especially a working man stuck all night in some small Midwestern town. He knew Rickie would rather be home with his wife, but the distance was too far to his hometown and not worth the ride since work started early the next day.

"Hey, man, let's go outside, get some air," Tyler suggested.

It was by the back trees when the offer was made. It was after Rickie had been prepped with how tough the working man has it and how unfair it is that some made so much money and some not enough, and that some people get a free house and some get no house at all.

"Yeah, you heard me right, an easy two thousand dollars for just a half-hour of your time. I just need help with a few details and to borrow the work truck for a short while," said Tyler. Tyler had taken out a small loan, since he now owned a piece of property, which would pay for the bribe that he told Rickie would soon be his.

Ty had created quite the elaborate story, all about Sarah and her homeless history, and Rickie bought it all, with the help of alcohol coursing through his veins. Small lies, Tyler was thinking, for a bigger truth, as he lied to himself. Rickie rationalized his actions while he talked in slurred words, also lying to himself about the risk he was taking. It did not take long for him to help Tyler get Everett's truck and drive out to Linnea's house site. They hitched the truck to the house on wheels while Rickie had some trouble standing, but the hitch was secure.

It did not take but half an hour for them to be heading back to the bar in Tyler's truck, which he had parked in a secret place earlier that night. Rickie had finally passed out after Tyler gave him a bottle of hard liquor for the ride back. Tyler knew his partner in crime would not remember much, even if Rickie would end up regretting it. The help Tyler had needed was not difficult even with a drunken assistant. Tyler doubted Rickie would remember the details, but if he did he would never tell anyone. Rickie would be in big trouble if he confessed: besides losing his job, it would be a legal issue if anyone knew. Feeling confident about his partner's complicity and about the house being correctly hitched to the truck, he left the poor victim sleeping in his own car parked near the bar.

Tyler drove back to Linnea's land and house, which was enveloped in darkness. There were no electric lights and no neighbors to interfere since the land was on the edge of town. He hid his truck again in the woods not far away and walked to the house as it stood solemn and alone. He thought about what he was about to do, about the risk he was taking. Before he could reflect more on his actions, Ty climbed into the house moving truck, and suddenly he was all jazzed. Instead of questioning his illegal action, he felt powerful and daring. So this is how it is done, he thought, this is how you steal a whole house on wheels. What a thrill! With the house hooked up and ready to go on the "borrowed" work truck, Tyler started the engine. The old Underground Railroad house was about to be on the move once again, except this time a thief with so-called good intentions was at the wheel, under the spell of a dark night.

Tyler drove slowly down the gently sloping drive and pulled out on to Oak Street and headed north, with no headlights shining from the truck. He was relieved it was an overcast night, with no moon to catch him in its light. It was one of those pitch black nights which gave the house a better chance of slipping away in the dark. Tyler turned left slow and steady and started driving down the long road of his planned route, away from town, away from watchful eyes. There were no cars in sight—he was alone with his stolen house.

The old house was moving on wheels as if it had a life of its own. Its nineteenth century past where it had been a part of breaking laws for a higher justice, for freedom, had been twisted in present time into laws now being broken for the wrong reasons. Stealing it proved to be easier than Tyler expected. In fact, he even thought it had been easier than it should have been. The house that had been hooked up to the truck was on the move. He was glad to be driving his stolen property. Without anyone except Tyler knowing it, a unique historical house was now "at large."

Since Linnea's land where the house had temporarily rested was already on the edge of town, it did not take Tyler long before he was on the country road driving westward to his land. He drove past a few farms set back quite a distance from the gravel road, knowing the farmers were long asleep. He had studied the route for weeks for his house theft plan, and he knew there were only a few wires up ahead where he would have to stop. The phone wire to one house would have to be cut, and the electric wire had to be raised, but he had it all figured out. Like many a thief, he was smart and quite observant. Had that intelligence been applied in other ways he would not be stealing a house down a country road in the middle of the night.

Tyler had once watched the house mover from a hidden place when Everett had first come to measure the house height. Sarah had mentioned the house mover would be in town, so Tyler watched from a distance as Everett used a pole of sturdy plastic pipe that could be extended in length, up to thirty feet, and then made compact as each section pushed inside the next. Tyler purchased just such a pole but not for measuring only. He figured out how to adapt it to lift the electric wire so the wire was not blocking his way while he drove the old house underneath. Then he hopped out of the stolen truck, and took down the pole so as to not leave any evidence behind. He also cut the phone wire blocking his way by standing on the truck to reach the low wire. He frayed the end of it to make it look as if the wind had blown the wire off. He did not consider that the farmer might need the phone for an emergency. He assumed the phone wire could be easily fixed and the farmer, thinking it was caused by the wind, would have his phone back on shortly.

Tyler again justified it all to himself, believing he was stealing a house for Sarah, a home that he thought rightfully belonged to her. Tyler figured if he got caught he would at least have his chance to say why he took the risk. It was out of his love for Sarah, he would tell them, and because Sarah had been homeless and she never had owned a home.

Tyler knew he loved her as he had never loved anyone except his daughter. At times the feelings were so overwhelming he would stop cold and forget where he was and almost who he was. Then he would snap back and become the practical carpenter he understood himself to be, a builder with wood, nursing resentment. Usually he pushed away the intensity of his feelings of love because at times it confused him, since his identity was more enmeshed with hers than it should be. But he knew he would do anything for her because of her innocence, because of her wounds. He would even steal a whole house for her.

So at two in the morning, before any farmers would be awake and with Tyler more awake and alert than he had ever been, he drove the truck with the hitched house at five miles an hour down the last stretch of road before he would turn into his plot of wooded land. The trees would nicely disguise the house, Tyler knew, while dismissing that the land given to him had come from his aunt's generosity. If he had been seeing more clearly he would have realized the land was an answer to a long held prayer by Sarah, and a gift of the heart from his great aunt for a place to build a house. It was not intended as a place for a stolen Underground Railroad house.

For Tyler the land was perfect camouflage, a hideout and respite site until he could spend the time it would take to not only disguise the house, but fix it up just the way Sarah had fantasized in her childhood. He would add white shutters on either side of the windows and put pink roses in the front of the house. Then he would add the beautiful heather Dutch door he had finished for her, waiting for the point in time when he would take history and twist it a bit, enough to create a house imagined by the woman he loved.

Tyler stopped at the entrance to his piece of property and cautiously turned down the dirt road with the stolen house innocently trailing behind him. He headed to the planned site where the grove of trees stood ready to hide his stolen item. He drove slowly as the house creaked on the road and seemed to shift a bit, or perhaps it was his imagination. Then he finally came to a stop after he placed the house as best he could in the opening he had cleared. Leaving the house on its wheels, he unhooked it from the truck. He felt certain no one would guess what he had hidden on his little plot of land. He stood looking at the house and smiled a bit, surprised at how easily it had all played out. His plan had gone exceedingly well.

Trusting the house was well hidden in the grove, he drove the truck back to town in less than two hours after stealing the century-and-a-half old home. On his way back he looked for tire tracks in the gravel that might give a clue, and then he would stop and get out of the truck and smooth the marks over with his boot. He then drove to town and checked on Rickie, expecting he would still be passed out, which he was, and left the keys to the house moving truck in his pocket. Then Tyler walked a few miles in the dark to Linnea's land where he had parked. He found his old truck with its shiny red paint, which he recently had repainted after he made a trade of his carpentry skills with an auto body worker. Besides having a nicer looking truck, it was a way he convinced Sarah he had to spend some of their savings, which in reality was going to the house for supplies. It also changed the color dramatically so people might not suspect it was him when he came in and out of his property.

Tyler felt relieved to be in his truck, after having executed his big house theft plan, and drove home knowing he would have to sneak into their apartment.

But deceit had become more commonplace these months for Tyler, so he was more accustomed to shifting from his role as a thief in the night to husband, father, and carpenter by day. Finally reaching their apartment, he went in quietly. Before falling asleep on the couch, he felt an uneasy satisfaction in stealing the house he believed belong to Sarah.

18

Shock

Who could ever imagine a whole house, with its tons of weight and formidable size, could be stolen? It was unthinkable, impossible, and just not doable. As Linnea stood before her tree clearing, completely alone, with the house utterly gone, she could not fathom what she was seeing, or rather what she was not seeing. How could her house be gone? Cars can be stolen, television sets stolen, even crown jewels are stolen, but not entire houses!

She could only respond with logic at first, thinking where on earth would a whole house be hidden, always an issue for any stolen item. The reality of a stolen house had an absurdity that bordered on humor, except now Linnea was in a state of shock. It was unimaginable that this could really happen, and part of her kept denying it. Her feelings were confusing and difficult to sort out, and her thinking was thick with disbelief. How could her house be gone? It cannot really be missing, she kept telling herself. It can't have disappeared into thin air. But on some level she knew she had to face that her whole house, in its entirety, had been stolen.

Because she was a doer, she wondered what action to take. Should she call the police? But how would she even make a report? Who would believe her? She heard herself on the phone to 911, emergency, imagining herself saying, "Yes, I would like to report a theft…of my house that was moved…yes…5512 Oak Street. Yes, officer, the whole house. Where? I don't have a clue…where does a thief put a whole house? When? I suppose in the dark of night."

Linnea thought it had to have been in the dark of night when someone with a dark heart decided to play a dark trick and steal her house of light. Who would do this to her? And how could someone steal an entire house? Everett had assured her it had never been done after one of the workers had joked about it. She could not get her thinking around the idea that it had happened to her. It was more than Linnea's logical mind could handle. The shock of it kept her breathing heavy and quick.

If her mind was in denial, her shaking muscles could not lie about the trauma. What her mind could not comprehend her body processed in its own way, trying to guide her. As her body became uncontrollable in its shaking she felt her world as she knew it was shattering. Nothing was as it was supposed to be, and her logical thinking was no longer a protective wall. Now with her house gone Linnea was left facing the emptiness she had tried to deny since her husband Ray had died.

The shock of his death, even if anticipated, had never left her. Until now her grief was so intense she had pushed most of it away. She had learned to package it up as if it were wrapped tightly in small boxes. Only one box could be opened at a time, and not often. But the veil had been lifted because of the stolen house and she had no choice but to face her buried grief.

Losing him had hurt Linnea and continued to hurt her in a way she never knew was possible. She did not think she could love anyone so much until Ray came into her life. He was the man she had waited to meet. As she came to know him she saw how funny and competent he was, and how full of warmth for her and for many others. He enveloped people with a sense of love and inclusiveness in his quiet way, while his humor kept him human and down to earth. Ray was liked by many people. He had a presence when he walked into a room that was commanding without being intimidating. He was equally comfortable talking with an elderly woman, or a business partner, as he was interacting with children. He had the kind of warm heart that pulled people in, as she had been drawn to him when they first met.

Linnea started to feel tears as they fell down her face, letting herself remember him. How long had it been since she had allowed herself even the gift of her memories? Why had she packed them away so tightly? She had more tender memories than she had wanted to admit because that would lead her to the loss that had left her feeling empty and too alone.

Whoever the thief was, Linnea thought, he or she would not have been able to do this crime if this person had known how she had struggled privately with the loss of her husband. While some anger at the unknown thief started to surface, Linnea instead resigned herself to her emotions of grief. She sat down now with her back resting on a tree, recalling times spent with Ray. They had experienced so much in their relationship, in the blessings and trials of a committed marriage. She even recalled their arguments, which she assumed were a healthy aspect of their relationship because she knew couples with honesty in their relationship are bound to fight at times.

When they argued, they each would take a stand with serious statements, until Ray would suddenly come up with some humorous line. Then she could not keep herself from smiling, even if she was reluctant to change her position in their heated debate. When she was ready to say something funny back, then it was as if the angels of humor had broken through a dark place in both their hearts. The tides were turned, and Linnea and Ray would continue their daily lives with fewer wounds to the heart because their humor had mended them.

It was painful to recall him and their history together. But memories flooded her mind and emotions. Linnea remembered when Blair was born, with Ray by her side, and just how vulnerable she felt with their infant child. She recalled being swept up with such love she could not contain it. The love she felt for Ray was expanded still further in her love for their daughter. It was the unconditional love of a parent for a child, a love that has no equal. She had never known more love than what she felt as a mother for her child, so interconnected with her love for Ray.

Now a thief had stolen not only from her but from Blair and from how they hoped to honor their memory of Ray. Stolen was the house with a promise to nurture and carry the remaining small family of two to a better place, a place of safety and comfort. The thief had stolen her security, her protection from the world, and her once-in-a-lifetime opportunity to live in a house she had moved by her own perseverance.

The thief had also stolen the protective wall wrapped around her heart that had kept her from experiencing her full grief. On this lonely, early morning while facing her house being stolen, she could no longer stuff her feelings into fragile, little segmented compartments. Now her grief came full force, without her permission, flooding her with triple losses. She felt the loss of Ray, the loss of a potential home for Blair, and the loss of her protective sheath around her sorrow.

Linnea finally wept tears that had been withheld for too long. With her body now curled and resting on an old oak tree and the earth sustaining her weighted heart, she cried in a way she never had. It was at first a soft cry, full of her memories of being with Ray. Then she felt the intensity of her pain near the core of her being, of the pain of her loss, and her tears streamed without her control of them. If the angels who watch over those grieving were looking down over Linnea in all of her sorrow, they could only know immense compassion for this woman, alone in her woods, without a home, without her life partner, weeping from the pain of it all. But such angels would also know for Linnea to heal, she needed to embrace the lessons that only grief can teach.

19

A Compassionate World

Linnea stayed at her parent's night and day for the last few weeks since her house had been stolen. The small stone cottage was her refuge as were the trees, which she now took the time to quietly observe. Those trees swayed with a rhythm that made her want to trust that her life might still have a sacred pulse and a reasonable worth and purpose. But it was difficult for her to trust that impulse when she was filled with grief. She was a wounded mother, like a deer injured with a fawn in need. She felt sorrow for Blair and her needs, but she could not meet them now. Her parents, grieving in their own way for their daughter, helped with Blair, as did Sarah who cared for her daily.

Linnea finally accepted her pain, which was exactly what she needed to do to heal. The walls that had fallen from her protective sheath let her weep as she never had, and in the presence of her loved ones. Grieving, with her parents or with Sarah present, helped her in becoming more attuned to the subtleties of her feelings, or the intensity of her grief work. Her parents gave her the stability she needed to accept her grief and Sarah stayed her trusted friend and a pillar of strength on which she leaned. She grieved with her mother and father as guardians and with Sarah as an anchor. It was this support which allowed her to go into the depths of her sorrow. And while friends may have thought her grief was about her house, those close knew she was finally grieving the loss of Ray.

Linnea depended on Sarah as never before, though Sarah had always been there for her, even in the innocence of childhood. Linnea felt swept up in Sarah's goodwill, as if the wind of the bluffs held them both suspended in the nurturance of the earth, in its rhythmic blue skies and the blessings of friendship. Memories came back, of Sarah with Linnea in shared childhood with wind blown dandelion seeds. Life was timeless and simple then, holding a quiet beauty Linnea had nearly forgotten. She recalled the wispy seeds floating up, appreciating the tenderness of those moments, cherishing them more than ever. Now she could embrace the sweetness of those days once shared in friendship.

With the tender memory of the seeds of summer, Linnea could integrate all the more the good she shared with her friend, Sarah, as well as with others. It was as if the sorrow of her grief gave back her sensitivity, which she knew as a child. The small, tender acts between human beings, unique moments in time, she no longer overlooked. She would notice the gentle smile or a simple gesture of kindness, both of which were more keenly observed because of her grief. It gave her an altered awareness of her world, as she realized how quickly time passes. This opened her to feel not only grief, but the beginning of grace and the sweet gift of gratitude. Such were the lessons her grief encouraged her to learn.

Her brittle shell had been shattered, and she was emerging, even if she was losing a part of herself. She was experiencing a death to a part of her identity and the ending of a life as she had known with Ray. It meant she had to grieve fully the loss of her husband. She had to grieve and let go of a part of herself and her life that would never be with Ray gone. It meant she had to find a new way to be in the world with a different direction for herself and her daughter.

Linnea spent many grieving days and nights in her family home, with the stone walls of the cottage as solid as her support system needed to be in order for her to grieve fully. Time for her was not measured in any way except by moment to moment awareness, be it of her pain or the sweetness in life. It was only then, after she began to emerge from her depths of her grieving, that she began to grasp what was happening around her. Sarah was the one to tell her first.

"Linnea, you are receiving letters and emails...you won't believe how many. A website was set up for you by Garret after he began receiving so many emails at his newspaper," said Sarah, concerned how Linnea may take the news.

"What do you mean—letters and emails?" she asked quietly in disbelief.

"I mean people are writing you from all over the country, and from all over the world. You will not believe how many," Sarah emphasized.

Sarah piled four huge boxes next to Linnea. "These are the letters—in these boxes—and I printed out the emails that have come to you at the newspaper, in the boxes here. There are more," Sarah added.

"I don't understand. Why are so many people writing me?" asked Linnea, confused.

"Well, it seems there has been a newspaper article written about the house being stolen. And now it's gone national. And—are you ready for this?—international. Your story is worldwide," Sarah said, wondering how Linnea would respond.

As it turned out, the Chicago newspaper was the front runner with her story. Garret had sensitively put together the story of a woman with a child, a widow well before her time, who had tried to start life over with a century-and-a-half-old house. And not just any house, but a house that was part of the Underground Railroad. The story of the historic house she purchased for one dollar, a house she had moved by her own tenacity — only to have it stolen from her and her daughter — had struck a chord with many people.

It was an unusual story, and people from nations all around the world were interested and compassionate. When people read about what had occurred in a small Illinois town near the Mississippi River, somehow the story resonated with them because of the loss, because of the injustice, because of the history. It was hard at first for many around the globe to believe that a house could be moved on wheels, and even harder for people to believe that it would be stolen. "Only in America," as some headlines read. But people saw the photos of a house on the move, and after reading the story, their hearts responded.

"Linnea, you have been getting letters everyday for the last few weeks. But since you haven't been to work, we — your mom and dad and I — didn't want to tell you too soon. We knew you needed time to grieve. Is it all right I told you today?" Sarah asked, worriedly.

"Yes, it's fine. Don't be concerned, Sarah. I just can't believe so many people would write us," said Linnea.

Garret had hoped to get the story in national news, not because he wanted the glory or any advancement. He knew America would want to hear this story. He knew people all over the nation would show their caring, and he felt it was the least he could do to support Linnea. He did not anticipate the worldwide response to her story and even he was a bit stunned.

He had not seen Linnea since the celebration. Garret had enjoyed meeting her that night, more than he expected. Because of his empathic heart he knew the disappearance of her house must have been a hard blow for a woman already dealing with the tragic loss of a life partner. It was not easy to write the story; he knew it had to be handled delicately. At times he felt at odds with the newspaper business because he saw firsthand the suffering of people, and making it public was difficult. Yet with this story he felt his skills in empathic writing and his potential role in helping were aligned. He was determined to try to help in a way he knew how.

What no one expected was the level of outpouring. Nor did they expect Linnea's story would hit so big nationally or internationally. Sarah had collected several thousand letters and emails for Linnea and more kept coming in daily. Emails arrived effortlessly on the world wide web. Letters came as if on wings, with messages of understanding from small, frail paper envelopes floating into Sarah's hands and into Linnea's heart. America's compassion, and the caring of so many people from other nations, was a true thing of beauty.

"Sarah, these are so tender. I can't believe so many people have taken the time to write. Who would ever imagine this?" asked Linnea in disbelief.

"It's remarkable. So many people care about what happened," said Sarah, still astonished.

As the story of a widow's loss and grief went national and then international, the heart strings of a people everywhere were touched deeply. Hearing that an entire house had been stolen, one with its proud history of Grace's great-great-grandparents who stood against slavery and of a people, be they white or black, who believed in humanity's inherent integrity, had people interested. Reading how a house sheltered the daring freedom seekers on the Underground Railroad that had gone forward and sheltered from birth to death four more generations with the promise of a fifth family kept people's interest. Other readers related to the story about Grace and Rolla Wolter who faced illness but were helped by Sarah, who did much more than clean, and of Linnea's story of a husband's illness and early death with all their money gone for a cure that never happened. Hope was inspired once more in readers with the promise of a new home in an old house for a mother and her daughter, a house they could buy for a dollar, a house they could move by their own tenacity and will so to start a new life.

Then the house with such a gifted history was unimaginably stolen by a blatant thief, robbing a mother and child of hope. America was stunned, the world was shocked. So opening their hearts and their own sorrows, citizens of the world gave of their kind words. Some gave even more: Many gave of their hard-earned money, from families well off and poor, of all races and religions. The donations came from generous souls who lived their truth of empathy and shared from their hearts and their pocketbooks. When multiplied, the generosity of money promised to create an abundance of funds that would give practical help to Linnea and Blair for part of the down payment for another house.

As Linnea read the emails and letters over the next weeks, the written words of understanding and caring sustained her in a way nothing else could. Not family nor friendship could give support in the way that a nation and a world community of heart-felt love could give. The transcendent sense of a national and global community filled her with awe and touched her as nothing else ever had. Because of the outpouring she was lifted above her personal circumstances. Even though they were strangers who wrote to Linnea and Blair, she could feel their genuine caring. They were all connected in a network of love and concern, and her compassion went out to the letter writers as well because of the many stories shared in gentle words of a loss in their lives. Either illness claimed a loved one too soon or an auto accident caused the sad and tragic loss. Linnea, along with her parents and Sarah, were touched by so many who shared their hearts and their sorrows.

"This letter is so sad. I never realized so many people have suffered in the ways I have, or how much we have in common with strangers," said Linnea.

"The letters are beautifully written. Many people have reached out," said Sarah.

"I know. They are touching to read," Linnea said, feeling less alone in the world.

"You can't help but feel a connection. People all over the world share the same sorrows, if only we could share more empathy everyday," said Sarah, wishing the world was a more compassionate place.

"I don't know how I will ever write back to every person, but I want to respond to each and every one," said Linnea.

"You will find a way, and I'll help. It just may take awhile," Sarah said confidently. Then she remembered a story from her past. "I experienced America's compassion as a child. When we were in shelters I recall people being kind to me. Did I ever tell you as an adult I wrote back to a shelter in Los Angeles to thank them and I sent a bit of money?"

"No, I never knew much about your homeless experience. I guess I never asked," said Linnea.

"I remember, once a woman took my hand, I must have been about six, and she walked me over to a box where I picked out a toy. I wasn't used to having something of my own. I still have the memory of how caring it felt when she held my hand. And I still have the toy, a little statue of a unicorn," said Sarah.

"You never told me that story," answered Linnea, surprised she never knew.

"I've known America's empathy first-hand. People help in many ways. I've seen people who care. Do you realize how much is donated every year to help?" Sarah asked her.

"I've heard we're a generous people," said Linnea.

"We are. We give in the billions of dollars, not only the government but the people." Sarah paused, thinking about her past. "Yet America also has another side. I've seen that harsh reality, being homeless."

"We're not without our problems," Linnea agreed.

"Like the rest of the world, we're full of contradictions. It's the same in many countries, the paradoxes, and the issue of haves and have-nots," said Sarah.

Sarah knew in her father's country of Bangladesh, many people were without homes due to limited resources and over-population. Sarah also knew that while Bangladesh was one of the poorest nations in the world, it was a lush delta region full of rivers from the snowmelt of the Himalayan Mountains. She had learned how generously many people in Bangladesh shared, even when there was not much to give. Her father had told her about going to a village where people who had little food offered it to him. To be polite he accepted, knowing full well it might be their last food for that day or more. He told her in a way a child could understand, that sometimes when people had so little it made them generous with what they had.

"I've always wondered how one of the wealthiest nations could have people who are homeless. It seems unjust in such a rich nation. I can understand the causes better in my father's homeland," said Sarah.

To better understand her heritage, Sarah had once gone to the local junior college for a slide show about

India, Bangladesh, and Pakistan. She learned about the 1947 partition of the subcontinent. What was once a whole region became divided and there was a mass exodus of many Muslims from India to East and West Pakistan. Bengalis, often known as the artists and writers from the Bengal region of the subcontinent, were separated by their religious beliefs into two lands. Decades later East Pakistan became Bangladesh in 1971 during a war of independence from West Pakistan, which then became Pakistan.

Sarah wondered about her roots, which felt distant yet always a part of her. She wondered what caused her Bengali father to leave his land of birth and start a new life in a different country. Sarah wondered about the suffering her father experienced when he was disowned because he married outside his race, against his parents' wishes. She wanted to know how he bridged two different cultures while losing his family link.

She thought about the many contradictions and complexities of her land of birth, America, and about the contrasts in her father's birth nation, Bangladesh. She thought of the wealth displayed on Michigan Avenue in Chicago, and the lack of housing for those without such means, be it in Bangladesh or America. She recalled the wealthy homes she passed as a homeless child and she wondered why the United States, given its abundance, was not a country where poverty had been eliminated.

Sarah knew Americans could be proud of their compassion. She had witnessed such empathy in her homeless past and in the current outpouring to Linnea. But she also thought that the shamefulness of her nation was poverty too common within its borders, be it a lack of food or homelessness. There was also the middle class working hard to pay bills, with the reality of homelessness just a few paychecks away if no extended family was there to help.

Still, Sarah knew many Americans, even with limited means and resources, shared as they could. She knew this growing up and again was witness to it with the letters pouring in. So it did not surprise Sarah as the letters were opened and read, that five-dollar bills would fall out from them, or small checks. Sometimes even larger amounts were sent, telling Linnea to apply it toward getting another home. The women were astounded at the number of donations and by the caring of many people. Even international borders meant nothing when it came to compassion.

Since no one in history had ever stolen an entire house before, the intrigue increased. Linnea started being asked to be a guest on talk shows. She was reluctant at first, having just emerged from such emotional pain, but then she thought maybe her story of renewed hope would help someone else facing a hardship, and the payment she received could go to a worthy cause. She went public and talked about the whole story, from the beginning of the 1853 Underground Railroad house to its theft in the new millennium. When asked, which was inevitable, who she thought stole her house and where the house could be now, she could only answer, "Someone out there knows, and eventually, I and the world will know."

She and Garret had spoken on the phone a number of times since he wrote his article, and she thanked him for his touching way of relating the tender details of her life. She told him she was glad it was him and no other reporter who first covered her story of losses and renewed hope.

Linnea told him how her life had changed, how she had to let herself grieve, how she had opened her heart to the suffering of others, and how she had the promise of another home. She said she had her eye on an old house, also threatened to be a teardown, which needed lots of tender, loving care, but she liked something about it, which defied words. Garret told her he understood that link with an old house. He asked if the house had to be moved and she told him not this one, and that she had enough to make a down payment where it stood. He wished her well with her new venture and told her he hoped they could stay in touch.

It was Sarah who brought Linnea the news of a further blessing. Another generous gift came in, one from a building contractor and his crew who specialized in renovating old houses. This contractor, from their area in western Illinois, had first heard the story on national news and after getting his crew on board, they all said they would volunteer their labor to assist Linnea in renovating the old house, with the contractor paying part of the costs of materials as his donation. Sarah smiled when she told Linnea, giving her that all-knowing smile, which spoke of the best of humanity. Both women felt enveloped in the goodness and generosity of people who kept reaching out. And it nurtured in them the will to find a way to give back, to share the compassion with which they were showered.

"Who knew the historic house would lead to such blessings? Who would have guessed?" asked Sarah.

"As painful as it has been, I would not have traded this experience for anything, except to have Ray back. I am sorry my house remains missing, and I'm sad Ray could not be here to see this outpouring of caring. But really, who knew such an enormous amount of good could come from such tragedy," said Linnea.

"Another one of life's paradoxes," said Sarah, smiling softly.

Both women, nourished with the tenderness they had discovered more fully in the world, were ready to step into their future. Witnessing the global compassion of so many people had restored a faith they almost lost because of the wounds of the past. They now knew not the worst, but the best of humanity, at their doorstep.

20

Hidden

As the nation and world responded, Tyler threw himself and his guilt, coated with resentment, into the rebuilding of Sarah's childhood fantasy house. He knew he would have to hide its identity, which he had planned with several construction projects to transform the look of the house. Before any altering of the house could be done he had to secure it, still on wheels, with blocks and shims so the wheels could not move. After he accomplished that task, he used multiple small jacks to support the house underneath all the beams and around the perimeter of the house. Once the house was stable, he took cinderblocks and placed them all around the house's edge so it looked as if the house had a solid, if fake, foundation. When he came up to a beam that was sticking out he used his welding skills and trimmed the steel beam. With stucco he added a textured surface over the cinderblock. He added wood to the end of each steel beam and covered it with stucco. As Tyler observed the finished results he realized he had created his first important step in house camouflage. It had taken him a good week's worth of effort, but when it was completed he almost felt a sense of pride.

Over the next week, he took off the glassed-in front

porch, knowing its windows had not been original to the house. The closed-in porch was not part of Sarah's imaginary house, and its removal was one of the easiest ways to change the look of the house. Instead he would add a simple railing and posts for an outdoor porch without glass windows. As he filled his truck with the refuse from the old porch, the shattering of glass and soft thunk of wood on wood were dissonant sounds in what was usually a quiet place. He took several loads of discarded material to a dump site and as he watched the refuse fall into a mass of waste, he stared at it, lost in thought, knowing he was one more step closer to disguising the Underground Railroad house.

This act of defiance against the old house exposed the door in the middle of the east side of the house. As in Sarah's fantasy her door was front and center. He removed the old door, another clue to the stolen house's identity, and he hung the beautiful Dutch door he had created with his own hands and vision, complete with Linnea's stained glass window. He had taken the beautiful hand-made, oval glass piece from Linnea, which she had created before she had ever dreamed of moving a house.

He told her he would put it in the door and keep it safely stored for their future gift giving. He knew full well he planned to put the door and the stained glass window on the stolen house. He did not allow himself to think of her efforts with the colorful glass window, let alone that it was her house he was defacing. For Tyler, the house was not honestly owned by Linnea because he was certain Sarah should be the deserving recipient.

Hanging the door was a solid day's work, completed on a weekend. He lied to Sarah about his whereabouts, telling her he was helping a friend with their house. Next was a larger project: working on the roof line by adding a false peak in the roof center, just over the door. This changed the look of the house dramatically along with the porch altered. He put new shingles on the entire roof, the materials he had purchased with a secret credit card unknown to Sarah, a card he was able to get given the value in his land. Replacing the roof was the more expensive and time consuming task, but he had saved money by buying at a huge building supply store, even if it had run the small stores out of business. He worked on the roof for weeks when time allowed him freedom from his job and mandatory family commitments.

To the edge of that new peak he added the lacey gingerbread, the fanciest fretwork from his company that he could afford. He had diligently applied several coats of white paint on the gingerbread while on a break at work. The purity of the white, called "pristine cloud," was perfect. This elaborate white-wood detail added to the deception. Tyler was sure this detail with the false peak and new roof shingles, along with the new Dutch door and outdoor porch, made the exterior of the house look completely different. He imagined if any witness to the new facade suspected the true identity of the house, he or she would be fooled now.

Tyler then took to the task of painting the whole house the soft, sky blue — or was it robin's egg blue? It was a color that was part of Sarah's memory. It was the color of blue that if looked at long enough could carry away all the worries of the world. With blue paint almost as thick as soft butter he covered over the ancient white clapboard of this one time haven for freedom seekers, as if the house itself had gone incognito, put into hiding with its true identity going underground.

Neither the unique history of the house nor ethics mattered to Tyler, only the task at hand of managing house subterfuge as quickly as possible, working diligently over a two-month period. After he was finished with the blue paint, he freshened up the white paint around each of the window frames and added the flower boxes that would become the recipients of Sarah's pink roses, ones she did not even know she owned. Tyler imagined roses that would smell pungent, triggering something good for her. He was counting on those pink roses to create a new memory for both of them when she accepted his remarkable and risky gift.

When he added the white shutters on both sides of the windows, he remembered her desire for security. As he stood back, eyeing her transformed house, he was certain he had attained this virtue for her, creating a place as secure as she had ever known, at least in the physical world. Never mind that the whole project was full of insecurities for him, because his sacrifice was not in question here. All that mattered to him was the house looking completely different from its nineteenth-century past and as close as was humanly possible to Sarah's imaginary house from her homeless history.

The more he worked at his cautious and painstaking game of house camouflage, the more convinced he became that he had taken the right steps. Although the risks of stealing a whole house were multiple, the camouflage was working so well on outside appearances that his internal world also started to suppress the fact of what he had done, of what harm he had caused other human beings. He also had stolen the historical authenticity of an important 1853 Underground Railroad house, stripping it of its architectural significance, but this he never even considered.

Parallel lies, of house disguise and hidden truths, became more deeply buried, even to his own soul's wisdom. He thought it was easier than it should have been to lie, even to himself. In his way of thinking, he asked why God, if there was a God, had not made it more difficult to deny the truth. It was so easy to pretend, to gloss over, to live in a fortress of denial. Of course no God he understood, nor Sarah for that matter, imagined anyone on earth would ever steal an entire, heavy house.

It was Sarah who knew God's signs were subtle hints, like quiet poetry, meant to be deciphered with intuition and body clues that whispered, "listen closely to the language of your soul." It was the gifted language of one's own soul with messages from the heavens softly hovering like yellow paired butterflies, until with a deeper listening, an inner voice strengthens. Sarah knew there always was the promise of an inner life full of intuitive knowing.

Tyler was removed from any gifted awareness or his intuition. He was blind to his inner world, which, if he knew how to listen, would always be available to him. It was a world waiting for his awareness where heaven and earth are integrated, in both the listening and an inner knowingness. A sacred place where prayer is song. But Tyler had bulldozed his softer nature along with his conscience, pretending the false ground was original soil, earth as it had been, the good earth as it was meant to be.

When he turned his ambition to the interior house, altering with gingerbread trim or his carpentry skills as much as he could, and then painting the rest inside, he kept on lying to himself. He said he was traveling the road less traveled. He said to himself, in his inner dialogue, this was meant to be, this house for Sarah. But a lie is always a lie, even if shimmed with hidden truths. And his inner world would not ultimately let him lie to himself. His soul was that good.

Yet soul-linking took time, and meanwhile Tyler was busy not only on his house deception but with trying to hide his associated actions. All his effort went to either hiding purchases it was not easy for him to disguise or keeping quiet the funds he needed for them. He paid for a post office box in the next town for credit card bills. He had to be cautious when he would sneak with a truck full of supplies to go work on the house. It took all the energy he had to keep his secret and to do the labor on the home. He often felt exhaustion and fear, manifesting as anxiety, but he was unwilling to admit it. He did not understand that the hurt in his body, even his fear, were ties to a lost voice, linked to his inner depth, whose whisper seemed silent, as silent as the dark universe at night engulfing a tangible fantasy house without light.

As his internal denial grew, his work on the house interior became a solitary focus almost like a meditation. As he painted the walls colors he expected Sarah would choose, he lost himself in the rhythm of painting. His identity began to merge with the colors and walls of a house he knew he deserved to give to Sarah. After such focused painting when time lost its boundaries, he turned his attention to the kitchen, which called for more brute force and an outlet for his tensions. Taking outdated kitchen cabinets from the 1960s and borrowing more money to put in new ones gave the kitchen a fresh new look. The updated kitchen meant he would need power to run the large appliances already in the house. Adding to his debt, he purchased a gasoline-run generator, which for now would supply their electricity. He knew many a country home had at times supplied a portion of its own power with such a generator, so it seemed like the least of his concerns. Down the road, he thought, he could add a propane tank, a windmill, even solar power, but for now a big generator would suffice.

Tyler kept working hard on the re-creation of a house Sarah would call her own. As he painted or sawed wood he found himself thinking about when she would first come to see the house. He imagined her standing before it, overjoyed at his accomplishment and loving it, loving him, without having any clue it was the stolen house. He could imagine her walking up to the door and entering it with her soft way of walking, as if honoring the moment. He thought he could almost hear her, as if with sacred steps she would enter the house with awe and respect. Or so he hoped.

It was this hope that kept him motivated and committed to a false truth. It was this hope he banked on, for a future with his wife secure in their home, with a daughter happy to the core. It was a propped up hope, full of caring and harm, of love and resentment, as he performed his unusual dual roles of house thief and magician of house disguise. With such obvious talent and huge effort he assumed he would now succeed easily with his tainted endeavors, with his house camouflage. This assumption, the fact he was so assured he would succeed in deceiving others, completed his self-deception as he went to work on the last finishing touches on the interior of the stolen house.

21

Secrets and Gifts

Tyler had invited Sarah out for a special dinner for just the two of them, so Sarah knew something must be up. Romantic nights out were infrequent with a child and a budget, and rarely did they happen at Tyler's initiation. As they sat at their table Sarah found herself relishing the atmosphere of the small family restaurant Ty had chosen in a neighboring town. It was known for its home-cooked food served family style, and people came from surrounding areas to share in the abundance.

Tyler was nervous about how he would explain to Sarah his fabricated story, but he was relieved by the softened dinner lighting. He had planned out all the details of his story, knowing Sarah had a naive side, which would help her to believe him. Sarah, on the other hand, knew Tyler was anxious about something. She could always tell by the roasted, smoky smell of tobacco which stayed on him without his realizing it.

Years back, after his daughter was born, he had quit his smoking habit, but on rare occasions he would smoke when he was particularly nervous. Sarah did not tell him immediately that she suspected something was going on, nor did she tell him about how she could tell by his smoky scent that he was anxious. She sat quietly eating her meal for some time before she spoke.

"So, what's on your mind? What's going on that you need to tell me?" Sarah finally asked.

"What do you mean? Can't a husband take his wife out for a nice dinner?" he questioned. Tyler hoped his wife's sixth sense would not uncover his plan.

"Yes, we can go out. This is nice, Ty," she said.

"Well, no point waiting. I do have some news to tell you. My great aunt left me something to inherit. Here's the proof," he told her, as he unceremoniously handed her a copy of the deed to the property.

At first she did not comprehend what it meant. Then she realized what the deed represented: a small plot of land had been left to them. Sarah was stunned. As she held the land deed in her hands she wondered how a thin piece of paper could mean so much. They were landowners now, with a piece of earth handed over to them with the same ease in which she had been put out homeless on the streets long ago. She started to feel as if the hope she privately held for her small family to have a home was now coming closer to being realized. With the promise of a plot of earth came the hope of a house they could one day build with their own hard labor.

"This *is* something, Tyler. Is this really happening to us?" she asked with uncertainty.

"Yes, it's real. I wanted to surprise you and Julia. But we do have a problem," he emphasized.

"There is a problem, okay," she repeated.

"You know how my brothers and sisters can be, with their jealous streak, as you well know. If they find out I inherited something and they did not, look out," he said.

Sarah knew that his siblings, although hard-working, seemed to feel scarcity was the order of the day. If one of them did a good deal better than the others, jealousy would rise up with a nasty righteousness. It meant Tyler and Sarah had kept their distance for years, even if occasional holiday meals were shared with extended family.

"We have to keep this quiet for a good while. In time I hope we can tell them, but for now we can't tell anyone, or my family will find out," said Tyler.

"You know I can keep quiet about things," Sarah said.

"I know. But you can't tell anyone, not Binnie or Leroy, and especially not Linnea, or it will not be kept quiet. You know she is open about talking to people, about everything," he said.

"Tyler, Linnea can be discreet," she stated firmly.

"I know, but she knows too many people, and if she slips and tells just one of them, this whole gossipy town will know," said Tyler.

"I realize she forgets sometimes. She'll be so excited for us. We finally have a place to build a house. Okay, I won't tell her for awhile. I'll ask you first before I mention it. I don't want any trouble with your brothers or sisters," she said emphatically.

"There is more. Another surprise. But I'd rather not tell you about this one. I want to take you out to the land tomorrow," he said matter-of-factly.

"Okay, tomorrow. I can't believe it! Are there many trees on the property?" Sarah asked excitedly.

"You will be in paradise. It's not a large piece of country property, but it's about three acres' worth of trees, set between farmland owned by two different farmers. The trees are a good wind barrier for the farm fields and that section never could be farmed, so the creek and trees were left alone. We have a dirt road, with a bit of gravel, which will be tough to deal with in bad weather, but it's the only land we can call our own," Tyler said, half smiling.

"Three acres seems huge. It was kind of your great aunt to think of us, to do this for us," said Sarah.

"She always liked you. And she seemed to like my woodworking. She said my great Uncle Verner, her husband, liked to work wood. We're lucky," he said.

"We're incredibly lucky," she said, almost in disbelief.

Thinking about their luck, Sarah reflected on how she had never owned much of anything. Now it seemed they had land, one of the most important things one could own from her perspective. A house to call their own would be some years down the road, but at least now it had become a possibility. It still seemed an unreality to her because she never had of a sense of roots in childhood, except for the time she lived with Linnea and her parents. Even then she often felt as if she were wavering between her homeless past, her mixed heritage, and the small Illinois town where she was loved. Her current joy, while evident, was still overshadowed by years of rarely feeling a sense of place.

Tyler thought their dinner had gone well. He could tell Sarah thought he had inherited land with no house, so he'd be able to surprise her again, but this time with more ceremony. He was also pleased she would be closed-mouth about it. He knew if she went and told people, and especially Linnea, that they had inherited property, everyone would want to come and see it. And just a few months after Linnea's house had been stolen, people could get crazy ideas, even if the house looked so different. He didn't want people sticking their noses into their affairs or uncovering his deception.

Tyler thought about the house and felt he had done well fixing it up as close to her childhood imagination as he could. He was as proud of it as he was fearful that someone would find out. He had not told Sarah about the white shutters that hovered over the pink roses he'd just put in planter boxes, under windows surrounded by powdery sky blue he'd painted on the house. He did not tell her about the Dutch door he had painstakingly made as close to her memory of her fantasy door. He did not mention the stained-glass window from Linnea's skills with a single glass rose in its oval center. He did not tell her about the stolen house or the lies to himself that had left him bereft of his own goodness.

He thought he had done well with the structure. He had carefully remembered what she had told him over the years about her fantasy house, and he had taken those memories and made them come to life. He took the imagery in her mind and added his own memory and like any architect and carpenter he created substance from ideas. He succeeded in creating a haven for Sarah, one she would indeed touch, putting hand to wood, so she could finally know her house existed in the tangible world. In his heart he dared for anyone to take away this dream of Sarah's, which he had managed to make a reality for her.

Sarah was pleased to know they would be going out to see their land the next day. Julia was on a sleepover at Blair's because of their dinner out, and the girls would be busy in the morning. While Tyler had wanted Julia to be with them, he accepted she was at Blair's. Linnea had told Sarah she was making efforts to give back because of the help Sarah had given with Blair when Linnea was lost in grief and unavailable as a mother. Sarah was looking forward to the morning drive with Ty to see their newly inherited property.

So the next morning came and they drove toward their land in Tyler's shiny red truck, which he had cleaned up just for the occasion. On the drive Sarah was thinking about the poems she had written about oaks and maples, and thought the old trees on their property would inspire future poetry. Maybe she would one day try to publish her "Tree Poems" out of respect for her "honorary" friends: oak, maple, birch, willow, pine, and cottonwood.

Somewhere out there she hoped a few people might be interested in her way of perceiving nature. She started thinking about the huge old cottonwood tree next to their classic Tivoli Theater, which was a tree with a trunk she had once measured at ninety-three inches around. While she was lost in thought about trees and the lush sounds of poetry, Tyler drove to their land. She suddenly realized she recognized a home.

"My friends Binnie and Leroy live just up ahead. I didn't know your great aunt had property out here," she said.

"I didn't either until she left it to me. Where do your friends live?" asked Tyler, concerned.

"It's this old farm house, coming up on the right. I have only been out here a half dozen times. I usually pick up Binnie in town at the library when we go on our adventures. Will we be neighbors with them?" she asked.

"Looks like we'll be country neighbors, within a few miles of each other," said Tyler.

"That just adds to the good news!" she said enthusiastically.

Ty was not pleased. It was too close for comfort as far as he was concerned, but he just stayed silent. He hoped they had not recognized his truck since it was a new color. He drove past as Sarah pointed out Binnie and Leroy's house, and a bit further down the road, he turned in on the dirt path leading to their property. He then stopped the truck before they were going to enter the woods that concealed the house.

"Sarah, I want to surprise you. Will you let me tie this bandana over your eyes?" he asked her hesitantly.

"You're going to make it a real surprise," she said, smiling at him.

With her eyes covered Tyler drove her up the dirt road. She felt the soft dust in the air leaving a faint coating on her exposed skin. It felt smooth as silk. While Sarah was kept in the darkness of anticipation, Tyler stopped his truck and slowly guided Sarah out of her seat. Without seeing anything Sarah could sense a large presence, but she was not suspecting a house contour. She could feel with her keen intuition something she knew was there but it puzzled her. Then Tyler, without saying a word to her, removed the blindfold.

There it stood — the dream house of her childhood, in soft pinks, blues, and whites. It was her imagination made manifest. Sarah was in shock. She suddenly felt slight waves in her body as if she might lose consciousness and faint. She questioned whether she was in current reality or in the memory of her imaginary dream. But as she stood staring at the house, she knew its blue clapboard and white shutters were an earthly reality.

Still standing in disbelief she could only wonder at how Tyler remembered each detail. She was acutely aware that he had taken what was fluid thought and fantasy to her and made them dimensional. How could this man have made it to order, just for her, and then gift her with it? She could tell all of his soul was poured into the making of the house, a home he so easily gave to her. It was the gift of gifts. She knew he, more than anyone, understood what this meant to her. He knew how deep her wounds were from her past homelessness, and he knew how her imagination had helped her to cope.

"I don't know what to say, Tyler. I can't believe what you have done," said Sarah, now staring at him with a stunned look.

"Do you like it?" he asked vulnerably.

"It's incredible. It's hard to believe," she said.

"Well, believe it. It's yours. This house has been here a long time but needed repair, so I thought why not fix it up like you dreamed," he said, smiling at her.

"So this is where you kept going these past months?" she asked.

"Yes, this is where I was hiding," he said, then wishing he had not said it that way.

"I'm trying to take it all in, to believe what is happening," she said slowly.

"Would you like the new key to your new house?" he asked tenderly.

He handed her a shiny gold key, a key he had been saving for this day, his house gifting day. As he laid it in her palm, putting his palm over hers, Sarah began to cry. Tears ancient with want and with grief from a past of longing for a home now fell down her brown cheeks.

Tyler knew she would cry and had come prepared with a cotton handkerchief with blue tatting on the edge that he had purchased at a local antique shop. On one corner was hand-stitched embroidery of a house surrounded by colorful flowers. Hugging her, he gave it to Sarah, showing her the detail.

"It's too pretty to cry on, Tyler. How in the world did you do all this?" she asked.

"You know I'd do anything for you. It was a lot of hard work. The house was not taken care of, but I brought her back to life. Go take a look inside," he said.

Holding on to Tyler, Sarah walked up the stone pathway. She felt as if she was entering a dream, as if Tyler had given her a house of light to fill a dark void in her. She first walked up to the windows with flower boxes and touched the pink rose petals, which felt like velveteen, just like the silky hands of her older friends, Binnie and Grace. Sarah leaned down so she could smell the rich and heavenly scent of roses. In a state of awe she then stepped up the few stairs leading to the Dutch door. Standing in front of the beautiful door she took her hand and moved it around the oval window of stained glass, and then touched the glass rose. How often had she, in her childhood imagination, merged with that perfect fantasy flower, how familiar its imaginary scent had been to her suggestive mind.

Tyler knew Sarah was moved by his efforts, and he told himself it was all worth the risk. As he watched Sarah's face slowly reflect a quiet joy, he was certain he had attained the best in house re-creation. He thought in a year people would have forgotten about the stolen house and then they could invite people to their home. He felt more assured that his secret would remain a secret, known only to his own soul, especially since it appeared Sarah hadn't a clue.

Tyler pushed open the top half of the Dutch door he had left unlocked to unveil the interior of freshly painted walls and old floors sanded new and stained a deep redwood tone. The oak grain of the floor planks was rich in pattern from ancient trees that long ago had been sacrificed so that many a person could walk upon that floor, be they freedom seekers before and during the Civil War, or future families living out their lessons and their purpose.

Sarah peered hesitantly into the interior of the house through the half open door. Like many of the houses in Havener that Sarah had been inside and dusted, the layout was familiar, with a parlor on one side and a dining room on the opposite. She knew the kitchen would be in the rear. She now wanted to explore every square inch of every room, but she also felt hesitant to enter her imaginary house made manifest.

After gingerly turning the key in the lock on the lower section of the Dutch door, she put her hand on the old brass doorknob polished near gold with hints of a copper sheen. She felt the cool brass and the texture of the knob design on her palm, as she smoothly turned the front door handle to her own house. It was a moment she never truly imagined could be real for her, as vivid as her imagination had been. It was a moment in time, without her knowing it, when her past and present collided into her future.

She walked alone into the interior, which felt familiar and yet completely new. Everything was painted fresh with plaster walls absorbing the colors of paint Tyler thought she would like. Soft greens like the color of her eyes lent a soothing quality in the living room parlor, with cream colored accents. She especially liked the muted copper in the dining room which she thought complimented the other colors chosen. It was all so perfect.

Sarah started to feel like a visiting guest, not an owner of such a lovely home, and had trouble envisioning living in such a nice house. It seemed to her to be spacious, though some might say, "What a cute little home." She knew it was all the space the three of them needed and the layout meant the house would live well. It certainly was more home than she ever imagined she could purchase or ever consider owning.

"Tyler, are you going to come in?" she called out.

"In a minute. I want you to have the house to yourself," he said loudly. He was overwhelmed and needed space to make the transition. The awareness that the house was stolen was no longer so repressed at the moment, and this kept surfacing in his mind as he saw her observe it; he thought it best to keep his distance.

When she walked into the kitchen with new cabinets and beautiful maple wood floors common in old kitchens, she knew she would especially love being in that room. The floors had been freshly sanded so they looked new but retained the charm of old wood. The kitchen windows had old glass in them, with characteristic waviness. She recalled Tyler once explaining to her that while glass appears stable, it actually slowly moves over time. After a near hundred years or more old glass looks wavy and shiny, distorting slightly the image seen through the glass. The wonderful views out the kitchen windows facing south, west, and north, with trees on all sides, had an illusion to them because of the waves of the old glass. It suited Sarah's perception, as she did not believe she could own a house with tranquil scenes out each window. What came easier for her was her willingness to embrace it as a house fitting into nature, in harmony with it. The green grass and the circle of trees around the house gave her a sense of spaciousness in nature. She had room to just be, to fully be herself.

"Looks like you approve of what you're seeing," Tyler said as he walked in the back door.

"It's unbelievable, Tyler. I don't know what to say," Sarah told him. "You are one amazing guy."

"I'm glad you like it," Tyler said, feeling a sudden release. He was a bit more relaxed now that he had her approval. This helped him to feel calmer than he had been in a long time.

"How could I not like it?" Sarah said and walked over to embrace him.

Sarah felt she had finally come home. After too many years of being uprooted, she knew this home is where her heart had always longed to go. She started to feel comfortable, at ease, warmly embraced by Tyler and by the house he had created.

"Go upstairs and see the rest," he encouraged. "I'll stay down here."

The house layout and stairway were similar to some other houses in Havener, so it felt familiar to Sarah. But it felt new as well. She felt curious to see more so she proceeded to go up the stairs with her hand on the old wooden railing made to fit well to the curve of her palm and fingers. Although the rail had recently been polished, the patina of the wood had a beautiful soft sheen from many years gone by. Sarah wondered who else had walked the risers of the old house staircase and what other hands had held the subtle but perfectly shaped wood banister. She was not imagining the many people who had escaped slavery and who walked up those very stairs to a bedroom for brief safety and rest.

Upstairs Sarah found four rooms with doors opened to a center hallway. The floors, which were wide pine boards, had been sanded and restained. The plaster walls had been freshly painted, an ice blue for one bedroom, creamy yellow for a second, and lavender, Julia's favorite color, for the third bedroom. The bathroom was painted a deep amber color. The upstairs view from all windows of the surrounding woods was even more expansive than the one downstairs. Sarah was truly in her element. She felt interconnected with the trees around her, which she knew were certain to inspire her poetry writing.

She could envision this house as a home to nourish her family of three—where they would sleep, dream, laugh, play, discuss, read, reflect, and be creative in various ways. She could feel how they would be nourished by the natural environment around them and how they in return would respect it. She knew the house would be a home where light would reign, where the sun would gleam through wavy glass windows, a light bursting forth with all that is good in the world.

The wisdom of the house started to whisper to Sarah, a wisdom that any house worth its weight in wood deciphers from the tree rings of life. The messages were about the goodness in her family and in their hearts and about the hope that remained in a world too often full of sorrow. Sarah was the fortunate recipient of a house full of wisdom and understanding, without her hearing the whispers of the true heritage of the house.

"Tyler, where are you?" Sarah called out as she walked down the stairs, with her hand gliding on the wood railing.

"I'm here, by the front door," he answered, ready to leave.

"I don't have the words to tell you what this means to me," she said.

"That's OK; you don't have to talk," he said, feeling uneasy once again.

"No, I have to say it. This house is the most incredible gift I could ever imagine!" said Sarah.

"Well, that's all I need to hear. That's why I did it. And I knew you would like the trees," he told her.

Just as she felt blessed by the gifts evident in the world of nature, she felt blessed by Tyler. He had given her a house from her imagination because of his unconditional love for her. It was a love she gave easily to many but now she was the recipient of such love. He had sacrificed and worked hard just to make her happy. He knew what her greatest need was and he fulfilled it. She finally had a house she could claim as her own, and it could never be taken from her. Sarah at last was standing in her house of light, surrounded by survivor trees, knowing she had finally come home.

22

Searching

Garret stood before Linnea at the newspaper office where she worked. He was seeing her for the first time since that ill-fated day of her stolen house. Although they had spoken over the telephone a number of times with a familiarity that surprised him, he was unprepared for the emotion he felt in seeing her. It was Linnea who broke the silence between them, a quiet that seemed to carry with it the weight of the past and the promise of the future.

"Garret, how are you? Long time, no see, as they say in Havener," said Linnea with a friendly smile.

"Hey, how are you doing? And how's your house coming along?" asked Garret as he gave her a brief hug.

"I'm hanging in there. As for the house, so far, so good. Of course, slower than anyone likes but that's an old house for you. It's a labor of love," she said.

Linnea's "new" home was in town, set between two older homes on a block with a brick road almost as old as the houses. She and Blair had moved into the lower level after the crew and developer had made good on their word to renovate, starting with the upper level. Plumbers, tile workers, electricians, and plaster wall experts spent their weekends renovating the bedrooms, and carpenters and painters laid their skills on the house exterior, doing far more than Linnea had ever imagined. It was a well-built home, as most old houses are, and the workers knew it was made of quality wood. Even if it was not filled with the history of the honored Underground Railroad house now stolen, it was a good, sturdy house, and it was coming back to life with the skills and efforts of many.

"Well, you seemed anxious for me to come down. I wanted to anyway, to catch up and to see your new place. Have you had any leads at all, about your stolen house?" he inquired.

"Binnie and Leroy—you met them at the party— well, they asked me to come out to see them. They wanted to talk about my stolen property. I thought you might want to come with, so I waited the few days until you could come down. You know, it might add more to the story—which, by the way was incredible, but I've told you that," said Linnea, feeling a bit shy.

"I was relieved the story went well. I'm glad you approve and glad it helped. So, when do we go see Binnie and Leroy?" asked Garret, enthusiastically.

"I set it up for this afternoon, after we go see my new—rather, my 'old'—house," said Linnea.

Garret and Linnea left to start their day together, catching up and talking in ways both had hoped. Their conversation was easy, even if they felt anxiety about the potential news about the house and a sense of the strong energy they felt between them. Linnea directed Garret who drove his car to her house.

After he parked they walked up the steps to a large porch and stepped inside her house. As they walked together into each room, talking about the progress thus far on her and Blair's home, she realized how much had changed in her life. She also became aware of how, in the midst of her transformation, Garret had remained in her life and appeared to be part of her changes. She watched him as he observed the details of the old wood trim. She liked his sensitivity as he rubbed his hand on the textured surface of plaster walls, painted in copper rusts and sea foam green. She was anxious to tell him more about their planned afternoon trip just outside of town, but decided to wait.

"What do you think of the house renovation?" she inquired.

"They're doing a great job. Look at the skill of the workers on the plaster walls. You have some talented volunteer workers on the job," he told her.

"It's nice to see an old house being taken care of, isn't it? I think more people would renovate rather than tear down if they understood just how solid and well-built old homes are. This quality of wood is hard to find these days. Our house is dated eighteen-eighty-two and the structural wood probably comes from the old pine forests in Wisconsin. The trim wood is walnut-all the interior doors are walnut as well," explained Linnea.

"It's a terrific house. The trim has a nice patina to the wood," he told her.

"I'm glad you like it. It's hard for me to believe it's mine, after losing a house," Linnea said, feeling suddenly uncomfortable.

"Not really lost, but stolen." Neither of them mentioned she had lost her first house after Ray died.

"Stolen it was. Can you imagine...how does someone steal a whole house? I still can't get over the nerve of it!" Linnea said, feeling incensed.

"Is it time to go see Leroy and Binnie?" he asked, wondering what would unfold.

"Yes. Can we drive out in your rental car?" she asked.

"By all means," he said and led her to his car.

Linnea did not know the couple, Leroy and Binnie, closely. Still, she looked forward to seeing them out on their farm, where they had worked hard for decades until they had retired. They were done with their tough working years of farming so they rented out the land to a nearby younger farmer. They still enjoyed seeing their land tilled and harvested. Linnea knew that Binnie and Leroy were mentors to Sarah and over the years she had heard things about them from Sarah. Linnea had been with them on occasions, observing the three of them converse. She noted their philosophical discussions, especially between Leroy and Sarah, which developed a depth most conversations lacked

Linnea did not know much about the past troubles this loving couple had experienced because of their interracial marriage. Leroy and Binnie had faced the discrimination of their day because they crossed some unspeakable line that by now mattered not to anyone they knew. It had been a firm line drawn by mis-understanding and fueled with contempt. But they had been determined to cross it. It had not always made for an easy life, but it strengthened their marriage because they had a bond and unity racism was not going to tear apart. So when Linnea and Garret were about to knock on the door of the old, four-square farm house, little did they know of the history, life struggle, and love that had occurred between this couple living between the walls of another old and worthy house, full of the integrity this couple had instilled in their home.

As Linnea knocked on the wood door, it was as if a slight echo came back to resonate in her body and connect her with the world in a bit more solid yet fluid way. She did not know what to expect to hear about her own house, nor did Garret, but both stood in the courage and risk of moving forward into the future. The door opened with the nostalgic creak of an old house.

"Linnea, welcome, come right on in. And this must be Garret. We met you at the party but I'm sorry we did not have a chance to talk much," said Binnie regretfully.

"Hello, it's good to meet you again, Mr. and Mrs...?" Garret's voice trailed off in question.

"Oh, please, call me Binnie. And this is Leroy," she said, as Leroy held out his hand.

Both men shook hands, with the solid, firm handshake that tells a person more than words can say. It was a ritual the men understood, utilizing body language to have an intuitive sense of the other man. Garret immediately liked Leroy, and Leroy, from that handshake, returned the sentiment, without either saying as much.

The conversation started about the trip down from Chicago, and then turned to the weather. Discussion of the elements, of Midwestern weather, was a given since it was so critical to farmers. Besides, it did take the edge off first meetings. Then they talked about Sarah, with Binnie asking how she was doing.

"You know Sarah, always learning, always thinking. She's quite the philosopher," said Linnea.

"Yes, she loves to talk universal and philosophical conversation," added Leroy.

Everyone smiled. They all seemed to know Sarah. At that, Linnea was ready to ask about the purpose of their visit.

"Binnie, you said you might have some information about my stolen house. I have been on pins and needles, wondering, but I wanted Garret to be here for this, so I waited for him to come down," Linnea said anxiously.

"It's not what I have to tell you, but rather Leroy. Just recently he told me something he had seen. We thought it might be a clue," said Binnie. "Why don't you tell her?"

"Well, very close to the time your house went missing, we had a phone problem. After checking the inside lines, I went out to check the pole, and sure enough the wire was down. I did not think much about it since, you know, we get lots of wind 'cross these fields. I called on a neighbor's phone for someone to come out to repair the wire," said Leroy slowly.

"Recently he told me about it, and I recalled reading in one newspaper following your story that wires must have been in the way when the thief stole the house. Leroy had thought the wire had blown down several nights before the house was stolen, but now we think it was that night," explained Binnie.

"So we thought it might be a lead for you, since you have had so little to go on," said Leroy.

"Tell her about the truck," said Binnie, pressing him to talk.

"Well, there is an old truck, painted fresh, that comes in and out of the trees just down the road a bit. We thought you might want to check it out," Leroy told her.

"Thank you for telling me. We have had so little to go on. It seems any tire tracks made by the stolen truck and house wheels had been covered over. This is the best lead we have had. We will check it out," said Linnea.

After strong lemon-iced tea and pound cake covered with fresh-picked raspberries and home-made whipped cream, they all said their goodbyes. Leroy clearly explained where to find the entrance, pointing them in a westward direction to a grove of trees in the distance that was not quite visible. Their search was on for the stolen house.

Driving west on the gravel road past the grove of trees in question, they decided to park the car further

down on an intersecting country road. They were
determined to sit and wait to see if someone might enter
or exit the dirt road leading into the grove. Garret had
a rental car, which gave a disguise of sorts, and bushes
on the roadside helped to hide them on an Illinois farm
road as flat as the eye could see.

"Linnea, I've been waiting to tell you something.
This seems like a good time to talk," said Garret.

"Please do," Linnea said, aware they were still new
to knowing one another.

"Well, since you tried to preserve your eighteen-
fifty-three house, and your second home is being
renovated, it started me researching about renovation
and energy." Garret was not sure she would want to hear
the details, but they had time to spare, so he talked on.
"I've been working on a new article."

"Tell me," Linnea was curious about what he
wanted to say.

"Well, it's a bit technical. I found a book by a guy,
Bruce Hannon, I think he's English. He coined the term
'embodied energy,' which means the energy contained in
a building. I've been reading how 'embodied energy' can
translate into BTUs per square foot," Garret explained.

"I know from a news article I read that a BTU is a
British thermal unit," said Linnea.

"And it's used as a way of measuring a "unit" of
energy. In the U. S. it's a way of talking about the heat
value and the amount of energy in fuels. So we can
translate into BTUs how much energy it equals to build
a structure," Garret said.

"You mean to build a house?" Linnea asked.

"Any building. In our country it takes seven
hundred thousand BTUs per square foot to build new —
that's the amount of energy used," Garret told her.

"That seems like a lot," commented Linnea.

"It is. What's interesting is some innovative people

are translating the BTUs into gasoline, like what a square foot equals in terms of gallons of gasoline. For a new building it equals ten gallons of gasoline per square foot," Garret said.

"Wow. Ten gallons per square foot." Linnea paused. "I think I can see where you're taking this. So if you renovate a house, it's equal to saving gasoline?"

"Yes, depending on how you renovate and by not tearing down, you save between five to nine gallons of gasoline per square foot. Some architects suggest we consider structures as you would think of valuable oil resources. Old houses are like oil reserves, if you will," Garret said.

"So renovating my house means I'm preserving oil reserves. That's good. One more good reason to renovate an old house," Linnea said.

"I'll have an article out soon for Chicagoans to read. I'll email you a copy," he said.

"I'd like that." Linnea was enjoying sharing their profession as journalists, and both with an interest in preservation. "Let's publish something in our local paper," she suggested.

"You have a deal." Garret paused, realizing he wanted to talk to Linnea in a more private way. He hoped to talk about his newspaper articles that covered her story and to know if she really felt alright about them. He first brought up the more technical article as it was less personal. As they waited he finally brought up the subject of the newspaper story about her stolen house. Linnea was able to tell Garret, in person, how much she appreciated his sensitivity in his writing. He was able to express how relieved he was that the outcome had been so favorable. As they talked they kept a steady eye on the dirt road. Finally their hour and a half of talking and waiting paid off. A truck was emerging from the wooded grove.

"Do you see the truck that's coming out, it's an old Ford and shiny red," said Garret.

"That's candy apple red to be exact, and that's Tyler's truck! What is he doing out here?" wondered Linnea.

"Is that him?" asked Garret.

"Not only is it him, but Sarah is in the truck with him. What in the world is going on?" Linnea said mistrustfully.

"Maybe they were visiting friends," Garret suggested.

"Friends I don't know about? Sarah and I know everything about each others lives. I can't believe what I'm seeing. I have to go in and look! They are heading east now, toward town, so we'll have time to drive in and look around," she said, insisting on her plan.

"I don't know, Linnea. Do you think it's a good idea? Technically, it's trespassing," he said cautiously.

"If someone is there, we'll just tell them we are lost, took a wrong turn. Happens all the time out here on these farm roads," Linnea answered.

Garret started the car and hesitantly drove to the nearby intersection. He could see that Linnea was determined, and he did not want to disappoint her. When he knew the red truck was fully out of sight he drove his car to the dirt road and turned down it. They were entering another world and both felt it.

"Let's park here, by these bushes. We can walk up further and see what we find," said Linnea.

Both of them got out of the car, feeling the cool evening air on their cheeks. They breathed the fresh crispness of an atmosphere from near summer's end that hinted of autumn, even though it was still August. They continued walking down the road without knowing what they would find, when in the distance they vaguely saw what looked like a small, unassuming house. They were a ways from the house, which was almost hidden, except for the distinct blue color showing through tree leaves looking like bits of puzzle pieces. Linnea's house had been grayish-white, so immediately Linnea thought this must not be her stolen house. They decided to walk closer, propelled by limited time and altering light. The intense dusk sky, emanating a lovely quality of radiant blue, was quickly turning darker.

Seeing the house more closely, in a small clearing surrounded by maple trees, oaks, ash, and a few cottonwood trees near the creek, Linnea could not imagine it was her house. In one glance she saw the entire front of the house was different and assumed the house was not hers. She knew there was some explanation why Sarah must have been leaving this house with Tyler. Maybe Sarah and Tyler had finally purchased a home but thought it would be upsetting to tell Linnea, given that her house had been stolen. Fear in her dissipated and warmth enveloped her, the warmth of the protective core that resonates in deep friendships. Linnea knew that when she experienced Sarah's embracing love; all felt right with the world. Any current doubts about her friend seemed resolved.

Linnea could now plainly see that the shutters and center peak were not of her house, and there was no enclosed porch, so she was certain this was not her home. She was not yet close enough to see the front door detail, the door Tyler had so lovingly made for Sarah, the door of wood sacrificed from an unsuspecting tree from an unknown forest. But when she did walk closer and see it, she stopped, with small waves of shock confusing her.

"Garret, that's the door Tyler was making for Sarah. And that's the stained-glass window I gave him to put in it. He and I were supposed to give her this gift together at Christmas," said Linnea, confused.

"So this must be their house," said Garret.

"Well, it's not my house," she said emphatically.

Garret stood center stage in front of the house in question. He observed the newly shingled dark roof and the center peak in the frontal roof line. He was suspicious as to the possible house behind the facade. As a reporter he'd been trained to always question what appeared to be the truth.

"Linnea, someone could add a false peak as a way to disguise a house, and take off an old porch. If we could go inside we could tell whether that roof peak is real or fake," said Garret.

"You didn't want to drive in here, and now you want to go inside?" asked Linnea, startled by his change. "I can't believe this is my house. It can't be," pausing to consider her next move. "I do have another idea as a way to check for sure. Before we moved the house, Blair and I carved our initials on the low side of the house, near the wood footing, around the left side."

On that past summer day, Everett had stopped work on preparing the house while mother and daughter made their claim and carved their initials into their home. It was as if some ancient script, set firmly into the old wood, was linking them to the Underground Railroad house, like a human ritual defining existence and bridging history.

Linnea walked to the far side of the house, with windows beginning to look familiar. It was then she started to doubt her friend, but she pushed away any sense of accusation because she told herself she knew Sarah too well. She could never take her house from her and thus steal her hope. Sarah could never be so dishonest.

It was Garret who discovered the cinderblocks were only slightly coated with a stucco concrete. The blocks were much looser than they should have been, and it did not take much prying for him to get a few free. As he shined rays with his flashlight under the house he saw light bounce off the house jacks holding up the house. It was when he saw the wheels under the house that he knew for certain: It was the actual stolen house. He did not want to tell Linnea directly yet because he was concerned about her reaction, so buying himself time, he asked her a question.

"Where about did you carve your initials?" he asked.

"It was about this far back. Can we pull out anymore cinderblocks?" she asked, standing next to him while he was on the ground.

As he did, she spotted something familiar and asked for Garret's flashlight. There, on the wood planks running horizontally, six initials were carved, clear as day. Six letters of hope. Consonants lined up in their dutiful way, their private initials betraying her certainty about Sarah, making her buried fear too vivid. It was their honed alphabet in wood that told her the truth and crushed her sense of trust.

"How could she do this to me, Garret? How could my best friend betray me?" Linnea asked him, anger spilling into her shock.

"I don't know. I don't know what to say, Linnea. I'm sorry," he said, stunned and angry to see Linnea put through such a charade. Who would make such a mockery of her grief? In his heart he wondered if Sarah could do such a thing, but he did not know her well. He knew from his line of work people attempt desperate acts. Yet because he was trained to think in questions, to always question, he wondered about what other scenarios could have taken place, who else could be involved.

Garret was aware that someone later might see the cinder blocks, so he quickly tucked them back in place. He was relieved that section of the house and the carved six initials were hidden by red roses.

Linnea by this time was sitting on the ground, stunned, angry, and hurt to the core. She could not fully absorb the idea that her house was found because she could hardly believe it had been stolen by Sarah and by Tyler. Linnea assumed he must have been a key player in order to pull it off. She started crying intensely while feeling angry. She lay on the ground, hitting the earth with her fists, while her fragile tears were small droplets, yet not inconsequential upon the earth.

Garret tried to get her up, but she would not budge. He did not want to watch her be so vulnerable, and he kept trying to raise her off the ground by her hand. But she needed the earth as her anchor so it could absorb the grief and rage that otherwise would overwhelm her. She stayed there until Garret finally crawled down to her and put his arms around her, two people huddled in the dark, as she wept and he consoled her.

"Linnea, let me take you home. You've been through too much. Let me help you home," he requested.

After a while, Linnea did not protest. He then walked her to the car, past the house that was once part of her dreams, but now had been sheathed with deception. The night air was cooler and the sky solemnly black as they drove down the dirt road and then on to the dark country road, with both Linnea and Garret in the silence of heavy sorrow. Linnea fell back into the grief from which she only recently had surfaced, but this time anger was laying its intense groundwork. She felt a silent rage she had not experienced with her husband's death, as her anger had been pushed back even further than her sadness. Now her rage was a current rhythm ready to sweep over her life, if she so allowed it to rule.

23

Betrayal

Betrayal was all Linnea knew. With her every thought it penetrated her heart with small, piercing arrows of deceit. Each painful arrow contained the magnification of Sarah's lies. Linnea could not fathom the deception of Sarah helping her to move the house and the hypocritical tenderness shown to Linnea after her house was stolen. The pain of her home being taken was a small fracture in comparison to the shock of Sarah's betrayal. How could her closest friend since childhood, who professed spiritual ideals, be so cruel? Sarah, the house thief, wounded Linnea's heart in lost friendship and damaged her sense of basic trust.

Was Sarah's need for a house so great she would betray a lifelong friendship? For Linnea no house was worth such a loss. It would be equal to giving up the chance to walk through green, lush forests on tranquil summer days. It would mean never knowing the light that filters through trees, or feeling the quiet repose that a forest or a good friendship offers. Linnea would rather have given the house to Sarah than to know this sordid, shadowy side of her friend or to feel such anguished pain in friendship lost.

Linnea reflected back on causes. She had tried to be careful in how she requested Sarah's assistance in asking Mr. and Mrs. Wolter. She was highly sensitized to Sarah's homeless past and understood she had requested a great deal of Sarah in having her ask for the house. That request being met was all Linnea wanted. She had never asked or expected more help from Sarah, who seemed to give it so willingly. Was it that first request that decided Sarah's plan of betrayal?

Did Linnea ask too much of her friend with a homeless past? Maybe she should have given Sarah the chance at the house first. Linnea examined her own motives. But during her reflection she felt an anger she had never before approached. It was a rage aimed only at Sarah who pretended to be such a giving friend while plotting against Linnea. With anger filtering into every doubt, Linnea wondered if she had ever known her friend. What kind of a person would be so cunning and so full of lies? What personality distortions were present, what hostile motivations? Sarah had seemed innocent enough. Now Linnea thought it was an innocence full of deceit and betrayal, and complete lack of authenticity.

Linnea and Sarah in the past had lengthy discussions about what it meant to be authentic and transparent. Sarah had read about Martin Buber's I-Thou relationship, and both women talked about their aspirations to achieve such genuineness in their friendship. Sarah had once explained Buber was a wise man who wrote about a sense of sacredness and mutual respect in the I-thou relationship. Both women discussed their desire to share this sacredness as friends. Linnea had experienced that rare interconnectedness with Sarah, but now she saw it as a sham of a friendship. Sarah was a con artist who was so good at deceit that she could profess empathy while stealing a house, disguising it, and keeping it a secret from her closest friend.

Linnea assumed Sarah had the initial idea to steal the house. She also thought Tyler must have been part of the entire plan because Linnea knew he would gladly go along with the deception. His betrayal was not nearly as hurtful because she expected less of him. She thought he would plot against her without much thought of consequences because Tyler often seemed lacking in awareness of his actions.

So anger and betrayal wrapped around Linnea's heart like a thick if brittle sheath, covering her heart's delicate surface. So penetrating was this rage that she realized she also could do the unthinkable. She also could betray Sarah in the most hurtful of ways. It did not take long for Linnea to devise her plan. It soon became a fixed idea that was her only focus, primary to her living. Linnea decided she would steal the house back. She knew this would hurt Sarah in the way Linnea had been hurt. It was a twisted lesson in empathy. Since Garret and she had discovered the house was still on wheels, such a theft was doable once again. She plotted it over and over in her mind. "I will steal my house back; I will do it," she repeated to herself under her breath. She was forgetting the gift from people all over the earth, and similar to Tyler, she was not considering consequences. Such was the power of betrayal's wrath.

She thought about the carved initials she had seen and touched that fateful night, her fingers on silken, aged wood, felt in the dark, initials that claimed the house as hers and Blair's, and no other person's home. Never would it remain Sarah's house. Linnea would never let her live there. It did not matter the homeless history of her former friend. It was such a joke that Sarah was her friend. Now she was her enemy, her foe, her challenge.

Linnea would return at night with Garret and a truck. Before the theft she would drill Everett for details, telling him lies about doing research for a book she wanted to write on house moving, a plan she'd explain to him would help her keep the current costs to house renovation covered. No one would know her plan of retaliation, not even Garret, until that night when she would sway him to help her. Then she would wheel the house away, stealing back the property that was rightfully her own.

Where would she put the house? There again was the issue of what to do with such a large, stolen item. She did not want to drive it back into town to her plot of land and risk others seeing her and the house. She did not want to be in her family newspaper, or any news for that matter; she just wanted to shock Sarah. A new location was not a big concern because she only wanted to move the house out of its current location, and it need not be far away for her to see the fruition of her plan. As long as the house was out of view when Sarah returned at night then Linnea could shock her with the house having vanished. What she wanted was for Sarah to feel exactly as she had felt that fateful morning. Linnea wanted her to know the same anguish when she drove to her wooded land and saw her house gone. Sarah would have to feel the pain Linnea had suffered. Even though Linnea knew she did not need the house, she felt it had to be moved to teach Sarah a lesson.

So the Underground Railroad house, once moved and once stolen, would be stolen a second time by its rightful owner. What of the consequences or the legal ramifications? What was a prison sentence for stealing a house back? Certainly Linnea could not be blamed for stealing, rather *taking,* what was rightfully hers. Maybe there would be issues of a lack of a permit for a house on the road, but Linnea realized she would not have to take it far. The house just had to go enough of a distance away from the road turn and out of sight on a moonless, dark country road. Then she could hide in the trees and wait and watch Sarah have the same anguish, torment, and pain that had filled Linnea when her house was stolen. It was the perfect plan of revenge for the betrayal cast upon their friendship.

Of course, Sarah was not the enemy nor was she the thief. Sarah never would have stolen the house and she never would have put her friendship with Linnea at risk. Stealing the house would not, and did not, ever occur to Sarah. She was as innocent of stealing the house as Linnea had thought she was guilty. It was guilt created from Linnea's assumptions. They were reasonable assumptions based on the lies of another, the real thief who laid false claim to a house, not out of criminal intent, but out of love.

His was an act hurtful to some but in irony it was a deed generated from Tyler's love for Sarah and a concern for her past wounds. He had a profound desire to amend her sadness and remedy her past. He took it upon himself to resolve the sorrow within her because she and many other homeless people had been lost on the streets of a nation that had forgotten its promise.

It was parallel to the lost promise of a once slave nation claiming all men are created equal when it was not the truth for any slave nor for women or most men at the time. In actuality those early words of equality were meant for men alone, and only those who could read and who owned land. But people over time changed that inequality. And the house that had been witness to the challenge of that lost promise of equality, a challenge taken by freedom seekers and abolitionists, was now a house that had become embroiled again in the issues of the times, be they homelessness or the emotional turmoil of betrayal and blame. If the walls could tell stories, many would be shared. This new story of betrayal and revenge, not worthy of the old house, had taken its course. Linnea was once again determined to achieve her goal.

24

Dark Night of the Soul

Linnea worked out all the details regarding her house move, except this time she'd be the shaker *and* the mover. She was sure she would shake things up with her hands at the wheel as she moved her house down the road. She felt excitement, mixed with anxiety, as if something powerful and intoxicating was taking hold of her typically rational choices.

She had been a bit unnerved when Garret called her and said he had gotten away from Chicago later than he had planned, but then she knew she would be asking a great deal of their new relationship. Linnea wondered if he would be willing to help her when he arrived, as she had not told him of her plan. She liked that he was a man of principle, that he had ethics in his career. Would she be asking him to undo his commitment to his integrity? Was she taking him down a fallen path along with putting her own future at risk? She wondered why she herself was willing to take this drastic act of revenge, which could put her and Garret in a bind with the authorities. But her sense of being the righteous owner of the stolen house kept her focused on her goal, along with her sense of betrayal by a lifelong friend.

Linnea had loved Sarah unconditionally and would have given to her in any circumstance. She told herself she would have given Sarah the house she was about to steal back if Sarah had truly desired it. But Sarah had never said such words, had never even hinted at a wish for the house to be hers. She always appeared satisfied to help Linnea with her house moving plans. Now Linnea knew it meant Sarah had plotted all along to make the house her own by stealing it from her closest friend.

Garret had told Linnea he would meet her out on the farm road near where the stolen house was hidden, where they had first stood watch. He assumed Linnea wanted to have another look at the house, so he drove more than two hours from Chicago to meet her. He had driven faster than he should on the smooth tollway westward past multiple farms and established towns. When he finally arrived he saw her car on the intersecting country road not far from the small section of forested land.

"Garret, I'm glad you made it," she said, hugging him.

"I told you I would, so here I am. What's the plan now, breaking and entering?" he asked, clearly joking.

"You understand it is my house; you don't doubt that?" she asked with intensity.

"You've proven it. But your tone isn't sounding good," he said, suddenly wary.

"She never should have taken my house," Linnea said angrily.

"No, but what can you do about that tonight?" he asked cautiously.

"I am going to teach Sarah a lesson. Walk with me?" she urged.

Linnea started ahead and Garret did not know what to do except follow her. They walked down the road with him trying to catch up, and then they walked together on the gravel road to where they entered the woods that hid the disguised Underground Railroad house. Linnea had rented a truck worthy of pulling the old, heavy house and had already parked it near the home. When Garret saw the large truck, he got worried.

"I just wondered if you could help me with the hitch," asked Linnea without emotion.

"You mean to tell me you are going to steal your own house back?" he questioned, shocked at her nerve.

"You bet I am! I've been planning this for weeks, ever since you and I found my house. I was just hoping you would help me with a few simple tasks, and I was hoping you'd take some pictures, you know, to document it. I assume you brought photo lighting for the dark," she said, using rational discussion as a distraction for him.

"I always bring light. But I've never been asked to help steal a house. I don't know, Linnea," he said, full of doubt.

Garret felt conflicted. His feelings for Linnea were growing, and he did not want to put their new friendship and potential relationship in jeopardy by saying no. He was having his own private struggle within himself. He felt caught between the woman he cared for and his own conscience. Ethics did matter to him, a great deal, but there was also the reporter part of him which was detached and thus wanted to witness and document the event. He found himself wavering, but leaning toward helping her. In a sense he thought Linnea had real courage to steal her house back.

"I just need a bit of help, with the hitch to the truck and a few cinderblocks pulled out of the way," she told him.

"You realize this makes me an accomplice," he said quietly.

"Not really. I am the one stealing it, but it is my house. I am just rightfully taking back what belongs to me," she said with conviction.

"Why not let the police handle it?" he asked, while starting to help her since she had already begun to pull out cinderblocks. He knew he was in over his head.

"They will be notified, just as soon as Sarah discovers the house is gone and learns the lesson of her lifetime. I will call the police then, I promise," said Linnea.

"What if Sarah and Tyler come home any minute now?" he asked.

"I happen to know exactly where they are. I have the timing all planned out, and things are going accordingly to plan," Linnea said, trying to reassure Garret.

So they worked as a team, pulling away more of the fake foundation blocks, thus unveiling the wheels that were still attached to the steel beams supporting the old house. Having better access to underneath the house both of them worked at lowering the jacks, which proved to be the most difficult task. Tyler had used many hydraulic jacks to support and stabilize the beams, but within an hour they had freed the house so that it rested fully on wheels once more. It appeared the Underground Railroad house would again be on a journey, this time down a dark road without a celebrating crowd.

"I've arranged for Sarah to be at my parents. They think I'm planning a different surprise for her, so I know when she will be leaving my mom and dad's house. By my watch we need to be pulling out now, so if you will help me with this hitch?" asked Linnea coolly.

The hitch was the easier task, with its ten-foot-long tow bar being relatively small in contrast to the house and its weight. The hitch itself was secured with Garret helping to lift it in place and making sure the link was tight. Linnea had already explained her plan was to drive the house west and then north while Garret photographed her pulling the historical house. She said she would take the house down the road and out of sight from Sarah, who would soon be driving back alone. The plan was to have Sarah discover that the house had been stolen from its site, with Linnea watching her from the woods, and then she would confront Sarah about what she had stolen.

Linnea climbed up into the truck. She felt in command of her life, feeling purposeful and in control. Any hesitations had dissipated into the adrenalin rush she was feeling. After checking both rear-view mirrors and turning the ignition, she pulled the heavy house slowly out of its temporary home. With a few cinderblocks toppling over and small sparks flying Linnea and her house were off and moving.

"Everything looks good, Linnea; just keep going!" Garret shouted.

So she did, as if the words were his blessing upon her planned act of revenge. She pulled the house slowly down the dry, dirt road, leaving brown clouds of dust on the trees that had kept the house a secret. The gravel road ahead shone a misty white from the truck headlights. Moving steadily but without stopping she slowly pulled out on the main road, making the transition from one road surface to another carefully. The house made a few slight sounds, of wood on wood creaking and the crunch of crushed lime stone, alternating with moments of silence and the barely audible sound of Garret taking multiple snapshots. Linnea slowly drove her house down the road as it became camouflaged under the dark sky and out of sight from the dirt road entrance.

Meanwhile Sarah, unknown to Linnea, wasn't driving out alone. Tyler had picked her up along with both Julia and Blair and they were heading west to their home. He planned to drop Sarah off, as she said she had to be back at the house, without saying why, by a certain time. Sarah had received some odd written message about Linnea and the stolen house, and she was told to be ready to go to Binnie's house at an exact hour. Sarah thought maybe Linnea would show up there, and not wanting Tyler to know, she planned on walking down the country road after he dropped her off. He said he would then drive the girls back into town and drop off Blair at her grandparents' home. Since he did not want Blair to know about the house, as he reached their long driveway entrance, he pulled the truck in and stopped without entering the woods so he could drop Sarah off. No one noticed the stolen house moving north down the dark road. Sarah had been talking with the girls and Tyler was focused on looking for the left turn.

"I'll leave you here. You'll be okay walking up the road?" he asked with concern.

"I'll be fine. I've got the flashlights you gave me, this and the backup one, Tyler. I'll see you later. Bye, girls. Have fun," said Sarah, waving.

The girls said their happy goodbyes as Tyler watched Sarah walk up the road and out of sight. Blair and Julia were quiet now as Ty backed his truck out onto the road. It was then he heard Julia shout about something in the dark, on the road behind them. She had been looking out the long, narrow rear view window of the old Ford truck. And now she was screaming.

"Daddy, there's a house, it's a house!" The house was lit up by the headlights of a car that was driving from the south. "Daddy, it's our house, moving down the road! Someone is stealing our house!" Julia shouted.

"Julia, people don't just go stealing houses," he said, not believing his daughter.

"Look, Daddy, it *is* our house!" she insisted.

And then he saw it in the distance, their house on the move. Never had it occurred to him that someone else might steal the house. It also never occurred to him that his own daughter would be the one to discover the house being stolen, the one he'd stolen first. In all his fantasizing about his own scheme and about how he would fix up the house as Sarah had imagined, it had never occurred to him that someone would have the nerve to steal it from him. He was almost incensed that someone would do such a harmful act to him and Sarah and Julia. But there it was before his very eyes: his house stolen and on the move down an Illinois country road.

25

Confrontation

Sarah stood where she first witnessed the imaginary house as a tangible gift to her. Now her gift had been taken away. Like so many times in her childhood, her vulnerability had been disrespected, her innocence disregarded. How often had she seen the beauty in life dismissed, its inherent good obstructed. Sarah was in familiar territory, with the potential goodness distorted by the limited understanding of human beings.

She knew, with the house gone, it had been too good to be true. She knew it was not possible for her to have been the permanent recipient of her fantasy dream house. She was so used to disappointment that even a house stolen, not once but twice, was not a huge shock to her. Yes, her house was gone, yes, another stolen house. Was it really any surprise that after one month of living in her home, long enough to love its unique charm, she would have it taken away? How often had she been displaced in her childhood years? This was just one more incident of being suddenly uprooted.

Still, she wondered why someone who intended harm and ill will to Linnea wanted to cause her the same. Why would someone want to hurt either woman? She had never done any act to hurt another human being, nor had Linnea, as far as she knew. Neither woman had ever done anything worthy of this crime. She felt as though the sorrow of the heartless had fallen upon the innocent.

This sadness was familiar. She had known it too often in the coldness that a dark night can bring to the body and soul of a homeless child. She was one of many left with the wounds from a world bereft of enough concern to take up each and every child into the warmth of heartfelt love. They were the wounds that stopped her from believing she could be the recipient of the American dream and a home to call her own.

Yet this sorrow had a sharp edge to it, because while living in the house, she had started to let herself believe this time she had a stable home for good. She had allowed herself to feel her roots settling, on her very own part of the earth, as if invisible chords were being sent down through floorboards into the very soil and clay beneath her, planting seeds to take root and grow. This sadness hurt in a new way because she was claiming the more empowered part of her being, which now was slipping from her as she felt overwhelmed with her current sorrow and past. It was then she heard Tyler yelling for her and he sounded worried.

"Sarah, where are you?" he shouted.

"I'm here, Tyler," Sarah called back.

"Sarah, our house is moving down the road. Julia spotted it. Get in," he said. As she jumped in the truck, he pulled back out on the main road and drove to catch up with their house on the move.

Linnea was still slowly driving northbound when in her rear view mirror she saw Tyler's red truck. It seemed an unreal image in such a small mirror, as if reminding her of the unreality of her past grief, which she once again denied by focusing on betrayal. Seeing his truck she realized she would have to change plans in how she would confront Sarah. She had to think quickly. She impulsively decided to just keep driving, to give Sarah a chase, as much as one can speed up while pulling the weight of a nearly thirty-ton house.

"Catch up, catch up!" shouted the girls.

Tyler was dreading what would unfold. He wondered what he had gotten himself into this time. He realized everyone would know his secret and he was as unprepared as any thief could be who is about to get caught. He was still thinking how unbelievable it was that someone would steal his house, as if he had some right to be shocked. Then he knew it must be Linnea, because she would do something this crazy. She had the determination to do it and the courage, just as he had. The difference was that she was the rightful owner to the house, even if Tyler could not admit it.

Tyler was quickly trying to figure out what he was going to say. Would he tell the truth or tell another lie to prop up all his other false statements? He did not like confrontation, dreading what would occur when they caught up with the house, but he knew if he left now it would be obvious that he was the guilty party. Wishing his daughter was not with them, he wondered how he would save face in front of her. He was leaning toward telling more lies.

Julia and Blair were thrilled and excited, if also a bit confused about a second house being stolen, this one in front of their very eyes. Both girls kept looking at one another, smiling, with their eyes wide in disbelief. How exciting it would be to catch the same thief that had stolen Blair's house, as if they were living in one of the mystery books they loved to read.

"Not one stolen house, but two houses! We have to catch this thief!" said Blair.

"And he's taking *my* house!" said Julia.

"Why didn't you tell me you have a house?" asked Blair.

"We were keeping it a secret until we had a big party to tell everyone. My mom and dad made me promise not to tell you. I wanted to surprise you at our party," said Julia.

"Oh," said Blair, trying to understand.

"We have to catch him, Daddy," said Julia.

"Catch that thief, catch that thief," the girls chanted.

Sarah realized they would not be able to find out who was stealing their house unless she got out and ran up to the truck window of the thief in question. She knew the heavy house was traveling slowly, only a few miles an hour, so she knew she could run and catch up.

"Let me out, Tyler, I'm going to run up," Sarah told him firmly.

"I don't think that's a good idea," he said, shaking his head back and forth.

"Stop, Ty, and let me out. That's my house someone is stealing! I want to meet them face to face," she said firmly.

It was not like Sarah to be this bold, Tyler thought. But he felt resigned to his fate, so he stopped. "Be careful," Tyler warned, feeling protective of her. "Use your flashlight."

Sarah jumped out, almost as curious as she was sorrowful that someone would steal her house. She wanted to see the thief who had taken both houses. Linnea saw Sarah in the rearview side mirror, running to catch up to her door. Finally Linnea would experience the satisfaction of the revenge she had planned so diligently, and Sarah would know Linnea had discovered the truth about the house. Sarah would finally know how her act of betrayal had hurt Linnea.

So it was on a small, western Illinois country road that Linnea in her truck, hauling an Underground Railroad house, was followed by Sarah, running, who was followed by an old red truck with a worried Tyler and the excited girls inside, and Garret watching it all while snapping photographs as the unbelievable drama unfolded. Having seen the house with their headlights, Binnie and Leroy parked their car and then stood in the dark of night in the cornfields, staying out of harm's way, watching and waiting to see what would happen.

All the differing realities and assumptions were about to collide on that fateful night, with truth meandering like a lost cause. What was not yet lost was the goodness inherent in the truth. As much as they each projected onto one another or disowned their personal insights, good rested underneath their assumptions, with the truth remaining the answer they were seeking. At the moment, Leroy was the only one who felt amused, not out of a lack of empathy but rather a fuller compassion that could take in human antics and the odd situations people created needlessly. He would have laughed out loud except he wanted to remain anonymous so he could watch the scene before him, knowing he might need to step in at some point and help.

The house came to a sudden halt. Sarah stopped running. Tyler put on his brakes. The girls were jolted in their seatbelts. Garret snapped a photograph. Then there was an electric silence, one quite familiar to the old house in its days as a secret refuge, a pause before life takes an unpredictable twist. Julia and Blair sat on the edge of their seats, as if watching in suspense through the truck window a movie scene at a drive-in theater. Time seemed to have stopped. The dark night grew thicker, the silence seemed to echo, and the stars in the night sky stayed as they always did — brilliant, complacent, and orderly. There was an absence of wind; stillness penetrated everywhere.

It was Sarah who started the clock of time again. She started walking toward the truck hitched to her house. As she took each stride she felt the strength in her long legs, as if each muscle and bone became aligned with the truth in the universe. She again felt her own power, as quiet as a poem and as powerful, with her spirit as strong as wind currents. She felt prepared for her future as never before. Her inner wisdom she claimed as if it had always been a known force to her. She knew, despite her past wounds, she could face this moment in time.

She suddenly saw Linnea jumping out of the truck, the truck that had stolen her house, the truck Linnea had just been driving. In disbelief, Sarah asked herself, why in the world Linnea would want her house?

Words started to fly from Linnea, as if accusations had the wings of night hunting birds. It was the kind of blame that crushes anything in its way. Sarah could not take in what she was hearing from Linnea, thinking there must be some huge misunderstanding.

"So, Sarah, how does it feel to have your house stolen!" Linnea yelled.

"It feels terrible, you know it does. Why would you do this?" Sarah answered.

"Why would I do it? Don't play innocent with me," said Linnea with complete mistrust.

"I don't know what you're talking about," Sarah said, genuinely confused.

"You know you stole my house from me, all the while pretending you were my closest friend. After all we have done for you in our family, how could you do it?" demanded Linnea.

"I didn't steal your house," said Sarah. The absurdity of it almost made Sarah laugh, but she was stopped by the intensity of Linnea's blame. Linnea went on and on, accusations wrapping around Sarah so tight, as if Linnea never wanted her to breathe again, desiring her to be so small as if to disappear. The more Sarah denied any wrong doing, the more Linnea held her accountable.

It was the final diatribe of accusations that gave Sarah her full voice. She defended the small turf of space around her, standing up for herself and defending her husband from what she presumed were false accusations.

"I didn't take it, Linnea. You're crazy for thinking I did. I would not do this to you, nor would my family," said Sarah.

"You took it! You know you did!" Linnea was certain she was right.

Sarah stood her ground as if she was a mother bear with her only focus being protecting her daughter and husband from harm. For one of the first times in Sarah's life, she stood firm, even against her dearest friend who had done so much for her. She held strong against Linnea's twisted thinking and multiple levels of blame.

Feeding all her attempts of shaming Sarah in a way that betrayed Linnea's delicate sense, Linnea kept on as if there were no end to blame's suffering. She had never in her life been this angry, this vehement in her conclusions. She was convinced Sarah had stolen her house, and none of the stated defenses by her former friend would alter Linnea's set pattern of thinking.

Two friends, who once shared sweet dandelion seeds during uninterrupted summers, stood at extreme odds. Never would either woman have imagined this fate, back when their small competitions had created temporary wedges in their early friendship. It had seemed they had transcended such issues long ago and had a shared closeness rare in friendship, despite their differences in culture, color, and temperament. But this wedge was insurmountable.

Leroy and Binnie entered the picture now, with Tyler still hiding in the truck with the girls, who fortunately were unable to hear the angry dialogue, though they could see their mothers were mad. Leroy spoke first, as a mediator.

"You two friends need to go off separately now and settle down," he said calmly.

"Yes," agreed Binnie. "You both have been through too much. Neither of you needs this grief. Sarah, you come over with me; you and I are going back to our house."

Everyone felt the aftermath of shame. Each walked in its wake solemnly, humbled by the trauma that humans cause. More than one person was trying to pick up the pieces of a sorrow that turned into unnecessary rage.

Sarah had heard all she wanted to hear from Linnea, and Sarah had stood her ground well enough, so she walked over to Tyler, telling him she would go back with Binnie. Tyler was relieved for the moment, saying he would take the girls back into town, as he wanted an easy escape until he could figure what he was going to do. Linnea did not see Blair or she would have taken her from Tyler. Sarah tried to reassure the girls that everything would be all right, after they kept asking her what had happened between their mothers.

Garret went over to Linnea, who was still seething. He just stood around in silence not knowing what to say to her and she was not talking. It was as if all the words she had spoken had been stolen from her, her words tainted, as if swollen with a false power that diminished language rather than gave it promise. Words could be so beautiful, she knew this, but hers had been ill-formed from buried anger. She was conflicted by her own behavior while feeling justified in stealing her house back. Garret, surprised at Linnea's rage, still stood guard, wanting to protect her and the house. He seemed to be the only one who realized someone had to call Everett and wait until the house mover arrived to again move the twice-stolen house. He expected Everett would be furious, and he understood why, given the huge risks taken. Garret decided he should be the one to wait until Everett arrived to handle an out-of-control theft of the Underground Railroad home.

26

Regrets

Tyler was pacing out back by the trees thick with leaves, and a woods that had once hidden the house he had stolen. His restlessness and fear overshadowed what residual defensiveness was left, and he knew he would have to come clean. He would have to tell Sarah the truth when she arrived on their plot of land. He would face it square on, he told himself, and tell her he had lied. He had to tell her because he knew he was responsible for his wife's sorrow that he had observed during the last few weeks since Linnea stole her house back. Tyler could no longer bear her grief about not having a home of her own because of his lies.

Sarah had stood her ground with Linnea ever since that fateful night when Linnea had stolen the house back, refusing to own any of Linnea's blame and defending her husband. He assumed she still did not know he stole the house because she kept giving him the benefit of the doubt. She kept telling him that the house was completely different so how could it be Linnea's. Knowing he had disguised the house created a tension inside him. His deceit was no longer bearable, nor was his dishonesty with her, or with himself.

He feared it would cost their marriage. He wondered now why he had not thought it through more carefully. Why had it not occurred to him it could all turn out this way, with the house stolen again, with his daughter as witness, and Sarah mourning the loss of a home? This only brought more injury to her earlier wounds of homelessness. It was her sadness and mourning Tyler could not handle, thus prompting him to ask her to meet him out at their land, so he could lay before her his act of deceit.

From a distance Tyler saw Sarah walking up the road to meet him. He in turn started walking toward her, willing to face the consequences of his actions, even if it meant losing her. He owed Sarah — and Linnea — the truth. With his denial finally lifting, he was beginning to see how he had hurt others and himself. He was starting to understand as he stole from someone else, he also was robbing himself of his integrity and his own belief in his abilities to create change in his life.

Just as Sarah had once walked to Linnea bearing the joy of good news, so Tyler walked toward Sarah as the bearer of the truth, with his whole body carrying the weight of his sorrow. What he did not realize as he walked toward her was that Sarah already knew the truth.

She had her suspicions about the house after they had moved in. How could she not? On some level she doubted the house in the short while she lived there, sensing it felt overly familiar. She thought it seemed too similar to Grace and Rolla's home she had scrubbed and cleaned, in how one knows a house only in the way cleaning can reveal a home. It felt as if she had seen the cracks in the kitchen wood floor before or somehow knew the living room floor corners with their bit of ground-in dirt. Yet the house had been put in such a new package it was easy to let it fool her. She did not want to face the truth of it being Linnea's home so she dismissed her doubts.

There were times she would tell herself the link between the houses was imaginary, but then it was as if the house was talking to her, trying to tell her it had been hidden, cloaked in false realities. She would then tell herself what an imagination she had, how her fantasy world had been part of what created her dream house early on as a homeless child. As Tyler's denial had kept him from facing himself and the pain he caused others, so did her denial of the most subtle of hints keep her from facing more grief.

She kept a secret almost hidden to her own heart as she assumed the right to live in the house. She was so accustomed to a home not being hers to claim that she felt comfortable with the cloudiness of that realm between conscious and unconscious awareness, which held the undercurrent of truth she simultaneously denied and realized. But in the realm moving from unconscious and conscious awareness, over the past weeks she started to admit that the imaginary house was Linnea's stolen home.

Sarah had to face Tyler and his lies, and she had to face her own role in what happened. She was an accomplice who, although she would never be accused in any court, had to face that she went along with the crime. She was complicit without him ever asking. She did it unconsciously to spare everyone pain, including herself. She wanted to prevent the loss of their home, even if it meant being a witness to a crime each time she looked at the walls of the house, living within the confines of a lie.

As Tyler approached, he was ready to tell her the truth, and she was ready to hear it. Both of them had matured as a result of a long summer too full of lies and grief. Tyler was standing in front of her, feeling vulnerable and in need of her acceptance. At first all he could do was stand before her with tears welling in his eyes because he feared she would walk away from him for good. Then he told her the truth.

"I took the house, Sarah, I stole it. I resented Linnea getting it when you had a homeless past and you didn't have your parents. I didn't mean for so many people to get hurt," Tyler said. He was genuinely remorseful.

"I know you took it," she said.

"You do know?" he asked.

"Yes, I knew awhile ago that you stole it." Seeing the pain on his face, Sarah added, "I know you didn't think it would turn out this way."

"I can't believe the risk I took and the people I hurt," Tyler knew he had hurt Sarah because she lost the first house she had ever owned. It did not matter they had a place to live after the house was gone, since they had continued renting their apartment all year.

"I knew you stole it but it took me some time to admit it to myself. I didn't say anything because I wanted you to come to me and tell me the truth. That's the only way you could start to heal, Ty," Sarah said softly.

"Well, I took it. I was so sure I was doing the right thing. I never thought anyone would find out, I was that sure of myself," he admitted. "I felt locked out of ever getting our own house."

"We would have been able to, in time. You have to trust more, in yourself, in life," she said, taking his hand.

"I know I do. I didn't think it through. You know how I can be. I act on impulse without thinking about the consequences," he said regretfully.

"Yeah, like where do you hide a stolen item as big as a house? You were bound to get caught," she said. As Sarah told him this, she realized on some level he must have known he would get caught, but he did it anyway.

He took the risk because of his love for her and Julia.

"I know you care about me, but you can't love me at the expense of hurting someone else," Sarah said.

"I realize this now. If it means anything, I *am* sorry for what I did. I was wrong." Tyler knew Sarah was right about love. He understood his devotion to her could not be at the expense of Linnea and Blair. "Sarah, I've been afraid I'll lose you. I wish we could go back in time, I wish I'd thought it through more. I never meant to hurt you and Julia, or Blair and Linnea. The last thing I wanted was to cause you more pain, or Julia. It's hard to face you with the truth because I'm ashamed," he said honestly.

"I know you did it because you love us," she said.

Who had ever been so selfless to her? If his methods were questionable, even foolhardy, he was giving in a way no one else had been. No one ever had loved her so much that an attempt to steal a whole house would even be considered, much less achieved, as wrong as it was. Then out of his love for Sarah he fixed up the house so close to the memory of her childhood imagination.

"If it matters, I was trying to make up for your past homelessness," he told her.

"I know you were," Sarah said, feeling as if she had not fully accepted the love he had for her until now. She wanted to be more open to his caring.

"How can I face my daughter with the truth?' he asked.

"We'll talk to Julia together. She'll need to know what you are doing to make amends, so she can learn." Sarah thought to herself how forgiving children can be, and as she had this thought she realized she could forgive Tyler.

"I'll make amends. I've already thought what I can offer when I go to court," Tyler said. "I'll do whatever I need to do to not lose you."

Sarah knew in her heart that Tyler was the one person who remembered the fantasy house that had been a comfort to her long ago, which he then created her dream into a tangible house for her intended happiness. He was wrong about stealing the house, but his desire to give was out of love. He took what was her childhood refuge during her homeless years and holding it closer to his heart than she to her own heart, he created her house, step by step.

"I have a forgiving heart, you know this. Ty, in a way it was a selfless act, to fix the house up like my fantasy. I don't want us to be apart, I want to work on things. We can grow closer through this," Sarah said.

"I'm sorry I hurt you," he said.

"Tyler, I forgive you." Sarah wanted to say the words directly to him. As she did she felt forgiveness wash over her, as if cleansing her. Saying to Tyler the words 'I forgive you' gave Sarah a new feeling of calm and she felt a vibrant love filling her to her inner core.

"Your understanding me and what I did, I can't tell you what it means," Tyler took both her hands and as he did he felt a sense of peace wash over him. When he looked at her he could see Sarah had something more she wanted to tell him.

"I played a part in it as well, Tyler," she admitted.

"No. You did not," he said, insisting on her innocence.

"There was a part of me that knew after we moved in. I didn't want to believe it myself, but in a sense I went along with it. I wanted the house so much; I didn't want to believe what I knew in my heart, that you had taken it. But that was before I realized one of the best lessons from all this: just how much you love me. I never knew anyone could love me so much," she said, holding both his hands to her face.

"I do love you, Sarah. I know it was wrong to hurt

Linnea and Blair, but I did it because I wanted to give you what you never had, a house and home to call your own," said Tyler.

"I know you did it because of my past. You always wanted to make up for my homeless history. You truly understood how much being homeless as a child influenced me, and still does. Wounds like that don't just disappear. And you came to understand how lonely it can be to come from two different cultures, from opposite sides of the globe. You have such a good heart, Tyler. But you will have to tell Linnea the truth, tell her all of it, and about how much you care. She won't believe me if I try to go to her," said Sarah with sadness in her voice.

"I know I have to face her. I already called Linnea, to meet with her. I will tell her what I've done," he said.

"She'll have you thrown in jail, Ty; she's not in a good place right now," said Sarah, knowing her friend.

"That's a risk I have to take. You know, Sarah, I have been thinking about Ray. It was hard for me to accept Ray's death. I've had trouble caring for Linnea because I could not deal with Ray dying. He and I were good friends, you know we were. I couldn't go to his funeral. I think I blamed her in a way," he admitted.

"It's been hard on everybody for Ray to pass on. I think Linnea is still angry and grieving. Now I'm the target of her grief," said Sarah.

"I do think she should have given you a chance at the house first. I am sorry, Sarah, for what I have done, but I have not changed my view about the house," he said honestly.

"What you don't realize is because of helping Linnea with the house move, I began to feel more confident about getting a house on our own. I'm feeling much stronger now, like I can create more of the life I want. That's freedom. It's not about getting a house for free, but it is about feeling I have the power to make a difference in my life. It was better for me that Linnea did not give it to me because I received a more important gift. The gift of my own power," said Sarah.

"I guess that's worth more than a house," he told her, half smiling.

"Indeed, as my father used to say, it is worth the immeasurable," she said, smiling.

After their open conversation and the start of a healing for Tyler and Sarah, they agreed to meet back at their apartment later. Sarah said she wanted some time alone to think and reflect, and she started to walk in her woods. Sarah knew she was embracing her ability to create change from her inner world. As precious as she knew each house could be, whether wood or brick, mud huts or mansions, desert tents or castles, she knew such homes were hardly equal to the human spirit that is empowered to be creative, whether to create a home or to create positive change in the world.

That sense of her power in the world, connected to a much larger sphere of love, was sacred to Sarah, as sacred as the wind, as sacred as the trees near the bluffs or the images of orange blossoming trees from her other homeland, and as sacred as the night stars from homeless nights. She realized now she was not homeless, because her spirit with its loving power, a spirit alive to the good earth, transcendent of national boundaries, was held supportively within the beauty of the world. She knew her home was the earth, blessed by glistening stars that were reflective of her own inner spirit. And she even knew, though her friend Linnea was distant from this understanding, that one day Linnea would embrace her own loving, inner world.

27

Gifts

Linnea had been introspective ever since Tyler had come to see her to tell her the truth about the house. She knew him well enough to know if he had apologized to her, then it must be the God's honest truth. Linnea had to face herself now, in how she had been so full of accusations and blame toward her dearest friend. Why did she ever doubt Sarah? She felt startled by her error of judgment, fueled by the rigidity of the constructs of her false logic and assumptions. Linnea was forced to soul search because her own sense of self and her whole view of her world depended upon it, not to mention her friendship with Sarah. If there was a friendship left to mend.

Tyler had been clear that it was his idea alone, that he never had help from Sarah when he stole the home, and that the house disguise was done secretly by him alone. He had even told her he did it all because he loved Sarah and wanted her to have the house from her childhood imagination, which is why he took the risk. He told Linnea he felt Sarah deserved the house more, but that now he understood it was not his to take, and that he had hurt her and Blair. He apologized for harming her and her daughter, saying he had never thought about the possible consequences.

Nor had Linnea thought it all through. She never imagined Sarah could be innocent. Linnea realized she had made one assumption after another about Sarah's guilt. She thought back and remembered Sarah had been patient at first with Linnea's blame, telling her she was mistaken. How could Linnea so misjudge this friend with whom she had shared blissful childhood days, overcome the trials of adolescence, and then braved adulthood together? She thought she knew Sarah so well, but she realized she did not understand the depth of her friend's caring, nor did she understand fully her childhood wounds and losses.

Even though Linnea did not say much to Tyler after he had come clean, she saw how fully he loved Sarah to do what he did. She realized even though he had been hurtful to Linnea and Blair, he had acted out of his devotion and his desire to help Sarah heal her past homelessness and the loss of her parents. Tyler had given Sarah what she truly needed. Linnea realized her own pain and sorrow had kept her from giving to Sarah what she needed most, a place in this world to call home. Linnea asked herself why she had not considered giving the house to Sarah, whose homelessness in childhood had left a haunting in her friend's heart. Tyler saw the hurt and sorrow and he did something about it, even if it was illegal, even at great risk to himself. He loved Sarah selflessly and was willing to make sacrifices. Linnea had known her longer, before Tyler ever knew her, so why was she not willing to be so giving to Sarah?

After Ray was gone, Linnea started to lose her connection to her more loving side; she could see this truth now. After his death the only thing she knew to do was to throw herself into her work and then into the house moving project, which continued her self-deception. But she realized it was even deeper than that initial hiding from her self. She realized she felt unworthy of the gift of the first house. She even felt unworthy of the gift of the second house, as grateful as she was for it. She also did not feel worthy of Sarah's friendship. She felt this way because Sarah was the most altruistic, loving human being she had ever known and she compared herself to Sarah. Because Linnea did not feel equal or worthy, she realized she had twisted the truth and found a way to make Sarah the untrustworthy friend, one who lied and betrayed. She projected on to her what Linnea could not own or face.

It was not intentional on Linnea's part as she had not understood her motivations until now. Realizing she felt unworthy of Sarah's love she understood why she was unable to give as generously. Now she knew without a doubt that Sarah would have given Linnea the house had their roles been reversed. Sarah loved Linnea so much she put aside her homeless history and her desire for a tangible home to help Linnea with her house move. Sarah gave to Linnea the greatest gift of friendship, the gift of pure love.

Linnea wished she had offered Sarah the house in the beginning. She could have given up the chance to move it and let her dearest friend have the opportunity. Another house would have come to Linnea in some way. She was living proof that a house could come from the goodwill of others, just as her current house had been given to her by the grace and caring of thousands who wrote her and sent donations. How could she have been so disrespectful of what others had done for her and then turn around with such contempt and focus her rage on Sarah? Such was the power of betrayal based on false assumptions and a sense of unworthiness.

Linnea wished she had been as altruistic as Sarah had been, but she hoped she could make up for the damage she had caused, which had only added to the sorrow of the earth and not its hope. She prayed she could begin to heal the friendship that she did not want to lose. She felt she could give freely and completely now that she knew the truth from Tyler about the house, and in understanding the truth about herself. She had been humbled into her desire to give fully.

Linnea knew what she had to do. She had to go to Sarah and give her the house. It belonged to her. Sarah needed it more than ever, given the horrible conflict she had endured with Linnea. Sarah deserved the house from all the trials of her past, of her four years of homelessness as a child, from being without her parents at an early age, and from her aloneness because she had to bridge two complex cultures: an ancient India and a youthful America. Despite all these difficulties Sarah had given to so many people, with such generosity in her heart that she had in her own right won the goodwill of the Underground Railroad house. She was worthy of the house with its radiance and embracing love.

Linnea asked Sarah to meet her by the house, leaving her a message through Binnie that she needed to talk to her friend. The former friends had not spoken since that night when Linnea had left her house on a dark farm road. The house had been pulled off the road that fateful night by Everett, who had a few choice words for everyone because of the risks they took. He pulled the old house back into Tyler and Sarah's land for temporary safe keeping until it was decided what would happen to the house. He thought it best that it was hidden back in the woods so to keep it away from people who would have been curious to see a stolen house. Everett did not want this part of their drama to be in the world news, because even if he was angry about the foolhardy risks they took with moving the house on their own, he still felt protective of both women. Besides, the quickest place to put the stolen house when Everett had been called up to retrieve it was back where it had first been hidden.

Linnea stood waiting in front of the house, observing the door with the rose of peach colored glass she had made for Sarah, aware of its fragility and its strength. She felt a cool wind behind her, hinting at the autumn winds to come, promising to bring with them transformation in the brilliance of color. In the death of one season would come the life in another in a never-ending cycle. Linnea thought of the fall and the last few days with Ray when the trees outside were full of fire oranges, deep burgundies, and creamy yellows. She still missed him intensely. It was not easy to face the seasons of change without him, but with love growing more generously within Linnea, it became a more peaceful task worthy of the lessons taught by life changes.

Sarah slowly drove up in the red truck. She had taken to driving it alone more and more on country roads, enjoying the expanse of the land and its tranquility. She parked, and as she stepped out of the truck and walked toward Linnea, Sarah noticed herself feeling stronger in her sense of place in the world, as if claiming it as her own, despite not having a home. Linnea, who noticed Sarah's more confident walk, started toward Sarah while feeling immense regret building inside her own heart.

"Tyler came and told me everything. How do I begin to tell you how sorry I am," Linnea said.

"Life can get complicated, I learned that way back," Sarah said, feeling a bit wary.

"I know it can, way too complicated. I'm just so sorry I hurt you in the ways that I did," Linnea said with even more remorse.

"I never thought you would do something like this to me. To take the house I thought had finally become my home, and to be so blaming," she said bluntly. The hurt she felt was obvious on her face.

"I don't know what I was thinking. I was so sure you had turned on me and taken my house," said Linnea.

She felt upset by the sadness on Sarah's face.

"You should have known I never felt as if much could belong to me, or that I would think I had that kind of power," said Sarah. "Plus you should know I would never do that to you."

"I know you didn't steal the house. I am sorry I ever accused you. It was because of my own issues. I don't think I ever felt I could keep up with you, with your intellect or with your ability to give so freely," said Linnea.

"Something good about homelessness and being poor is that it can make you generous. When you have lost everything, what does it matter? Material possessions become insignificant next to human suffering and a need for compassion. I think my father knew this from his family turning their backs on him and disinheriting him. He knew what values were truly important to him. Compassion is an ancient wisdom from my Indian heritage," she said proudly.

"I know, Sarah. You have always had a certain wisdom about you. But I could never seem to be as wise or as insightful, and I compared myself to you," Linnea said honestly.

"I never wanted you to compare yourself. I always accepted you as you," Sarah said.

"I know you did. You have been a kind of teacher to me, even when we were children. And once again you taught me something about friendship, about forgiveness. I have forgiven Tyler. I understand why he did it, how much he loves you. And I think he is right about the house. I was not as giving as I could have been to you, and to myself. I have to work on that, on forgiving myself," she said.

"You have to forgive yourself." Sarah paused, and then asked, "Do you think Tyler was right about the house?"

"I do. I think he is right that you should have had the first chance at the house. I could have let you have it and something would have worked out for Blair and me," Linnea assured her.

"It would have been hard for me to take it — because of Ray," Sarah admitted.

"Ray's death had a lot to do with my choices," Linnea confessed. "With Ray gone I felt panicked — and that I had to do something to feel more secure. I think my grief over him was distorted into many other feelings because I found it hard to grieve. When the house was gone it did help me to finally let down and feel my pain, but I still felt betrayed by life. I felt he never should have been taken from us so quickly."

"His passing did happen fast. No one was prepared," Sarah said, with gentle compassion.

"I never knew loss was so complex," Linnea admitted. "Now it's better because it's as if Ray is not completely gone. I guess I have learned many lessons."

"Well, if it makes a difference, you made me grow as well. I have never stood up for myself like I did when I was up against you, and that was good for me. And seeing how you took charge in getting your house moved, I could not have done that in the past. But I'm changing. I feel more empowered to pursue my ideas and make things happen in my life, to not just accept my fate," said Sarah.

"I'm wondering if you can accept something that is your fate, your destiny," said Linnea.

"Depends," said Sarah hesitantly.

"I want to give you the house. I want you to have the Underground Railroad house that I stole and that Tyler stole, the house I thought you stole. I want you to have it," said Linnea.

"You want me to have the house, to keep it here?" Sarah said with a smile.

"Will you let me give you the house?" Linnea asked.

Sarah thought for a moment. "It's easier to accept it now than if you had offered it in the beginning," she said reflectively. "Isn't that odd? It's as if we all had to go through that entire storm in order to learn our lessons."

"I think I am learning mine, big time. Will you take the house?" Linnea asked again.

"Will I accept your gift? I will take it, if it means we will be friends again. It was terrible not having you in my life," said Sarah, reaching out to her friend.

Both women held one another in a familiar hug that meant all the more to them now that their friendship had nearly been lost. The tears in their eyes continued the mending in their hearts.

"No one knows what we have been through as friends on this incredible journey. I don't want to walk this road without you," said Linnea.

"And I want to share my home with you, and I've so many ideas to share. I can't believe you are giving me a whole house! And I don't even have to move it; you did that for me," said Sarah joyfully.

"With Tyler's help, we got you this long-awaited house. Of course it had to be cleared with the judge because of the legal issues of my moving the house without a permit. Actually the judge thought the whole story was somewhat amusing, but not for long. You know I just came from court. Tyler was there." Sarah did know and Tyler told Linnea she could tell Sarah what happened. "I was given community service, like Tyler. He got the maximum number of hours and I got close to it. Ty did seem really sorry. He knew he hurt all of us. I felt lucky because our judge kept everything about my stealing the house confidential," she told her, knowing the consequences could have been more severe.

"You have close to the maximum community service? The house was yours," Sarah asked.

"I see how unsafe it was for me to steal it back. Someone could have been seriously injured or worse. And I hurt you. At least she let me keep the house. The judge could have taken it away from me. But lucky for us, the house is fully mine to give," Linnea said.

"After everything we went though to move it, I'm glad," said Sarah, remembering all their plans and work.

"She knew I was going to give it to you, I told her in court. It's a beautiful house, Sarah. I'm so glad I can give it to you. And I can't believe Tyler could fix it up exactly like your imagination—he's talented. The judge told him he has to teach local people without homes some carpentry so they can learn a skill and get work. He was fine with the court arrangement."

"He'll be helping people, I'm glad. Smart judge. Tyler did do a good job on the house, even if he altered it. As it turns out, the porch was not original anyways. Binnie and Leroy did some research. It's just that false roof he added that changes the architecture of the historic house," said Sarah.

"The judge thought of this, too. She had an expert speak in court and the agreement was for Tyler to take off the false peak." Linnea was glad she could tell Sarah that both she and Tyler were trying to make amends. "And the judge said she would like to see your home be open once a month for people to tour it, since it is historic. She also said, even if the color is not historical, the next time you paint, maybe you can change it."

"Sounds fair to me. And you know I'd be happy to share my house," Sarah said.

"I remember when we were kids you used to draw pictures of your fantasy home," Linnea said.

"The house had a way of staying with me. I'm glad it will look similar to the original Underground Railroad house. Wait 'til Blair and Julia hear about us getting the house," she said excitedly.

"They'll be so glad we're friends again, as will my parents," Linnea said.

"And Everett." Sarah added.

"He had to testify in court, you know. He was *not* happy about it. You should have heard him yell at me about moving the house," Linnea said, regretting her actions. "He told me he wants to be saving and moving old houses, not dragged into court!"

"Binnie and Leroy were not happy about our conflict because of our friendship, and the historic house. They said they couldn't fathom us *not* being friends," Sarah revealed.

"Well, we are friends, I hope. As a friend I took the liberty of going in the house and I straightened up, though most of your belongings were fine. The house was level. It still surprises me that not much inside fell when the house was moved, and on a gravel road. That tall six foot lamp that stands in the corner—it didn't topple over. Everything stayed level, so the furniture and your things were fine. Your dishes were in the cupboard, just as you left them. You had a few items slip off some tables, but thank goodness nothing was serious," said Linnea with relief in her voice.

What Sarah did not yet know was when Linnea had cleared with the judge about giving Sarah the house, she'd also arranged for the home to be further stabilized until a permanent foundation could be poured. "Shall we go in?" Linnea asked quietly.

The women friends walked inside the house. Sarah was flooded with emotions as she re-entered her stolen house. Both women sat down at the kitchen table, in the room Grace Wolter once said was the center of the home, with light shining through the old window glass. Sarah and Linnea started talking about everything, and both shared their feelings of joy and sorrow. In that same room many a conversation had happened over the centuries, when a brave goodness within the hearts of many a person was manifested. That kitchen had heard the stories of freedom seekers risking their lives for the promise of freedom. It was as if the stories from the determined souls who sat in that kitchen and were kindly given warm food could nourish a family from another century.

Now those kitchen walls, infused with the good history of a wonderful old house, would bear witness to Sarah and Linnea's lessons. Both women continued to talk about how they had changed. At times they were tentative given what had happened, but they had been friends for so long that it did not take much time for them to be sharing their thoughts openly. Sarah had numerous ideas she wanted to tell Linnea, especially about the research she had done since her conversation with Leroy and Binnie. She decided to share what she had learned.

"I have so much to tell you. Leroy and Binnie taught me some terrific things about history and I've been reading books. Did you know the Underground Railroad was the *first large scale* civil disobedience movement in America? Leroy told me." Sarah asked.

"No, I never knew," Linnea said.

"And you know Henry David Thoreau, who wrote about civil disobedience, well, he was part of the Underground Railroad," Sarah told her.

"And I didn't know he was involved," said Linnea.

"I researched a story of him helping a man escaping slavery, Henry Williams, who arrived in Concord, Massachusetts on foot from Virginia," said Sarah.

"Did he make it to freedom?" Linnea asked, knowing so many stories were lost about people who escaped slavery.

"He did, he reached Canada. They say Thoreau helped many people escape—more than any other man in Concord. He refused to pay taxes because he opposed slavery," said Sarah.

"I always liked his writing," Linnea stated, glad to hear Sarah sharing openly with her.

"I'm excited because I'm discovering links. I've been reading about Gandhi, I mean, *Ghandiji*, the *ji* means respect," Sarah explained. "He used to study Thoreau and his writings about civil disobedience. Thoreau used the term civil disobedience—actually he first wrote 'Resistance to Civil Government' but changed it to 'On Civil Disobedience.' Thoreau's work had a strong influence on Gandhiji. This links the two times in history."

"I know about civil disobedience but not the connection between the two men," Linnea responded. They sat at the kitchen table and shared ideas almost as if they had never been separated. "I know Gandhi started a freedom movement in India."

"Ghandiji saw civil disobedience as resistance to injustice and done without violence. I'm so fascinated by this history," Sarah said with enthusiasm. "Gandhi thought you should be willing to die for your beliefs but not kill for them. One of the ideas I love from him is being fearless and yet acting so no one is afraid of you."

"This research must be meaningful to you," Linnea said, knowing how important it would be personally for Sarah.

"It is. I'm learning about India and Bangladesh, where my father lived as a child. I hope to visit one day.

I'm seeing ties between the two different cultures." As Sarah spoke she had a sense of how she had grown while she and Linnea had been at odds. "Gandhiji was born just four years after the end of the American Civil War. He worked in South Africa and he stood up for Indian rights there. Then he went to India and started another non-violent movement," Sarah explained.

"I know about India, but not Africa," Linnea responded, realizing she wanted to know more world history. She also felt aware of how she missed sharing ideas with Sarah. "I never realized there were links between India, Africa, and the United States."

"And there is a link to the civil rights movement because Martin Luther King studied Gandhi and his use of non-violence, and now you know Gandhi studied Thoreau," Sarah went on. "I love all the interconnections."

"So it links India and America again and two different centuries," Linnea added. She wanted to be caught up in the ideas, trying to put their past conflict behind them.

"And the Underground Railroad movement was a precursor to the Civil Rights movement, so Leroy explained to me," Sarah said as she smiled.

"I never connected the Underground Railroad with the Civil Rights movement. All these surprising links. You've been doing great research!" Linnea said, pleased that her friend had this to occupy her during their recent difficulties.

"It helps me with my personal history. I know more about my roots and I see how I'm linked to this greater human story," Sarah shared. Hungry to share her thought, she added, "There's more."

"More? How can there be more?" asked Linnea.

"It was a complex time in history. The movement for women to vote was one more civil disobedience movement," Sarah told her.

"Another civil disobedience movement? " Linnea asked.

"Another one," Sarah said. She felt how easily they slipped back into a comfortable feeling of friendship even if it felt new in a way.

"I remember reading women wanted rights, including property rights," stated Linnea.

"Women wanted rights from the start of America and a few states finally had some, but many did not. Women who opposed slavery assumed if they fought against it, then they would get their rights after slavery was abolished. Many put aside suffrage to help the abolitionist cause. Of course for black women, both mattered," Sarah explained.

"I remember learning the fight for abolition gave women a chance at leadership, yet they were criticized for speaking in public. It's too bad it took so long for women to be able to vote nationwide," Linnea said.

"I wonder how our country would be different if *all* women had received full rights in the 1700s? And how would history be different if slavery had never been allowed in, and if we had respected American Indian tribes?" Sarah questioned.

"I wonder what a history professor would say about you, Sarah, being from this small town in Illinois. You ask good questions! And do you know, you've linked together two centuries, three continents, *and* four different civil disobedience movements. You have been busy!" Linnea exclaimed almost in disbelief.

"How about that for a little girl, once homeless and wandering the streets," replied Sarah, pleased with her efforts at research and with her friend's admiration.

"I'm so impressed. I don't know how I ever imagined I could live without your brilliance! You have a wonderful mind," Linnea said, reaching over to hug her friend.

"Well, you don't have to live without me because we're friends for good," Sarah told her as she hugged Linnea back. "If we survived what we've been through and if we can weather the house being stolen twice, I think we'll be friends forever."

"I hope so. I missed you," Linnea said.

"I missed you too much, even if I was upset. And I missed talking about ideas and all this history!" Sarah knew there were not many people with whom she could share so much.

"I have something to help us share more ideas." Linnea pulled out an old, dark leather book and handed it to Sarah. "Grace Wolter sent me the original diary with a letter telling me I could have it to keep. She also asked me to be sure and share it with you. Even in Florida, she heard about our falling out, and I think she hoped this would get us talking."

Sarah held the book in her two hands with reverence. She knew reading the actual words about the Underground Railroad written by Grace's great-great-grandmother was a rare opportunity.

"Grace and I decided the original copy should stay with you and the house. We both want you to have it. I made several copies already, for our historical museum and one for Blair and me, and Leroy and Binnie, but we want you to have this one," Linnea said graciously.

"I don't know what to say," Sarah said quietly.

"It's very moving to read. I have highlighted the references related to some of the passengers on the Underground Railroad, written in different places in the book. I guess I've done my own bit of research. This diary tells an important part of the story here in Havener," Linnea shared.

"Do you mind if I read it alone? I'd like to have a

little time to take in everything that has happened. It's not everyday a friend gives you an eighteen-fifty-three house, and a historical diary!" she said.

"Can we meet soon? I don't want to lose you now that we are friends again," Linnea admitted.

"Of course we can meet! And you won't lose me," Sarah assured her.

"You're certain about that?" Linnea asked.

"We're life-long friends. Count on it." Sarah told her, while giving her a loving hug. "I'm just a bit overwhelmed and need some time to be alone. I think I will take a walk and sit in the woods to read the diary."

"You always did need time to be quiet," Linnea recalled. "I'll leave you, for now."

"And I can get reacquainted with my home!" Sarah added.

"And read to your heart's content," said Linnea, waving goodbye as she walked out the back door.

28

A House of Light

Linnea walked away feeling a lightness of spirit with each footstep as she left Sarah with the gift of a permanent home. Just as Sarah had said she enjoyed delivering the dollar bill to Grace, so Linnea loved being the delivery woman of a house first created in Sarah's imagination. Linnea felt the full joy of offering a home to Sarah. It was good to be giving, and Linnea felt gratitude for being in such a position, because of people all over the world, where she could give away an entire house.

The residue of guilt, carried because of her past accusations, continued to dissipate as she walked the good walk. With Sarah able to forgive her, now it was Linnea's task to fully forgive herself. Sarah's understanding of the anguish caused by Ray's death helped Linnea to feel tenderness toward herself. She knew such self-nurturance would help her heal the wounds of the past and to trust in the friendship Sarah reassured would be life-long.

Instead of heavy guilt Linnea started to feel a sense of her own integrity because she had saved the Underground Railroad house and now gifted it to Sarah, along with an important historical diary. Linnea allowed herself to feel some pride again in knowing she helped to save the old home from being torn down, expecting the sturdy house would exist for another one hundred and fifty years. Everett explained the house would last once it was put on a new basement and foundation. The house was just that well-built.

As Linnea walked, Sarah stepped outside the house that once existed only in her mind but now had become her permanent home. Seeing Linnea walking in the distance, Sarah headed in a different direction, looking for the solitude of the woods surrounding her well traveled home. She began to walk by her favorite trees, stately in their presence, feeling the hush of a soft breeze in their leaves calming her. She held the old diary in her hand as she walked deep in thought. Then she turned to look back at her new home with its beautiful wooden door, complete with a peach colored rose. As she observed from a distance the gift of her blue house with white shutters and the glistening oval glass in her front door, she again was surprised at how remarkably close it came to the haven she imagined during her homeless days.

Never had Sarah fantasized that she once again would be able to actually see, much less live in the house of her imagination. Yet this historic home had been offered to her freely and willingly. Linnea had come through in a way Sarah knew her friend was capable, even if it took her some time to arrive at that centered place of giving.

Sarah reflected on all that had transpired since the once ill-fated house was threatened to be torn down but instead had survived to become a teacher to them all. Its lessons were for the heart, to test how much truth and caring the people who walked inside the embrace of those strong walls could discover within themselves, be it in current times or centuries past. Her house with its soft blue clapboard siding and surrounding pink and red rose bushes, seemed to hold a solemn promise, as it had from a century before. It would remain a house of good will, one that had supported many a person in his or her searching, even when it meant the law was broken — either by passengers or conductors on the Underground Railroad making claim to a higher law — or by a man in the twenty-first century who acted out of his love and a desire to heal wounds from Sarah's homeless past, even as he had to face his own deception in the process.

As she walked amidst trees, Sarah felt ready to read the handwritten journal begun nearly one hundred and fifty years before. She decided to sit with her back resting against a tall evergreen tree. While smelling the uplifting scent of pine needles, she slowly opened the book, feeling the fragile pages under her fingertips. The almost translucent indigo ink was written in a beautiful script. Each entry was signed at the end with initials in light, delicate lines:

M.G.R.W.

Sarah noticed most of the marked entries were short, though not all of them. Each one was dated and each told part of the story of the Underground Railroad house.

The Diary

Sept. 3, 1853

We have had the honorable opportunity to assist our first passengers on their journey to freedom. They were a family of three whom otherwise would have been torn asunder. My heart poured forth, especially for the young child not but five years old, and my conviction is growing stronger in partaking of our actions, whatever the consequences. M.G.R.W.

February 12, 1854

I have cooked extra biscuits and gathered up whatever supplies I could, including a much needed blanket, to send off with our last visitors in need. It is a small comfort we can offer, but I am glad that all my efforts and my cooking can see a fruition that serves a higher purpose and cause. M.G.R.W.

July 31, 1855

We give praise there is a Canada and a north star to follow, for only north is it safe for those upon a journey for their very lives, out of bondage. We give praise for this humble house that is a haven for the brave souls who find passage here. Four more people were hidden this last night and all day today until the evening. My husband showed them where to hide under the bottom of the old wagon covered with hay and he took them to the next safe house, a near twenty miles from here to there. M.G.R.W.

Sept. 15, 1855

When I asked our last passengers about their
life on a plantation, sadness grew in my heart.
One mother told me of her many children
she had seen sold off to slavery and her grief
was difficult to contain. How remarkable is
this brave woman! Would I have had her
strength? I would have had to, due to the
injustice which must be stopped. No mother
ever should have to undergo such torture.
Humanity must learn another way, for no
person should be treated as she has been thus
treated, with contempt. My commitment to
provide a haven is fortified after hearing the
story of those whose names I must not write
so to protect their identities. Still, their names
will always remain hand prints on my heart.
M. G. R. W.

January 7, 1856

If I could have a vision of all the invisible footsteps upon this solid, wood floor, of the
footsteps of passengers of courage, I would see
the vision of a promise. With such a vision it
would be my hope for all those footsteps to mul-
tiply one thousand fold to our home, and to the
many safe homes across our Illinois land.
M. G. R. W.

June 23, 1856

I have not yet written down about our red glass window. It is an oval shape and we light a candle by it, and the rose light from it shines forth so passengers know this is a safe house. The small window is by the stairway landing, on the north wall. This is the sign, a secret our house tells to those with a need and desire, that this is a place to stop and take good rest.
M.G.R.W.

Sarah stopped to reflect on what she had read thus far. She felt inspired and moved by reading such personal words about a difficult time in history. Grace said that her relative, the very woman who penned the diary, had wanted to be educated at Oberlin. Grace told her it was one of the first colleges in America to admit women. Sarah thought the author of the diary had a way with words—without a college education. She wanted to read further to better understand history and the individual story of a unique family willing to take risk after risk. Sarah was hungry to read the words about those who took the ultimate risk and dared to seek freedom, with words put down by one woman who took her own risks. Sarah wished she could read what people who were escaping would have written if they could have. But they had been forbidden to read and write, though some learned despite the unjust laws. Sarah felt well aware of how many words had been stolen during that time in history. This diary was one of the rare windows into seeing first hand the workings of the Underground Railroad.

March 27, 1857

Another family in need of shelter arrived, a
mother with her children but without the father.
Because of concerns for their safety they had
to part from one another in Alton, by St.
Louis. How difficult this must have been for
them all. We gave the mother and her two
children warm clothing and gave them soup,
when not much later in the night we heard a
knock on the door. The escaping family hid
in the other room, just to be certain, but when
we heard the code word "friend," we opened
the door. As this man spoke to us, the woman
rushed from the other room because there before
us stood her husband! This is a day none of
us shall forget as we rejoiced to see this family
reunited. As they are presently rejoined we
pray they stay together, safely on their way to
Canada. M.G.R.W.

August 29, 1857

I held a black rose of a deepest burgundy color,
a full blossom, in a cream-colored vase. I
walked quietly to the room where the woman
passenger, close to my age, was resting. I
knocked and she answered the door without fear
because it was the code knock, and I entered
and gave her the flower. She looked at me with

such kind eyes and with wonder at the flower.
She told me what a delicious smell it has and
she held it for me to partake. In that moment
I realized if times were not as they remain,
we may have become dear friends. There was
a rapport, a kinship beyond words, while we
both knew the black rose symbolized a permanent farewell. When I see those black roses in
bloom each year I shall remember her, hoping
she reaches safely to the end of her journey to
freedom. I will think of the friendship that
never can exist, except in our hearts and our
memory. M.G.R.W.

Sept. 14, 1858

The risks have increased yet they are more
paramount as we are closer to war, which
appears to be on the horizon. Yet our private
sacrifice in our home is small if we compare
the risks of those we assist, who chance their
very lives in the name of freedom. I recall
each and every person who has come through
our door, searching for a new life. What
mighty determination! We sometimes hear
word when someone makes it to freedom in the
promised land of Canada. Praise for the
answer to our prayers! M.G.R.W.

August 20, 1859

I weep for my nation as it struggles and is torn apart with the threat of separation, and fear running like a wild horse. I weep and pray for this nation as it struggles with itself and civil war looms. M.G.R.W.

March 19, 1860

We would not have thought as many as fifteen seekers would arrive at our door-step in such cold, but we took them in and shared what warm food we had. We asked of a neighbor, who had previously been opposed to helping but who recently has seen the light, and he loaned us not one but two horses, since our horse was lame. We now have safe transport to the next station. Praise Be! M.G.R.W.

September 22, 1860

Let us not forget the good people, of both races, who will have to fight this sad war soon to be upon us. While we do not abide by killing another human being, it seems the nation knows no other way to stop the wrongs of slavery. All will be held in my prayers. M.G.R.W.

November 24, 1861

It continues, the unfortunate repeat of history, the bloodshed of war. We wish there to be an end to all war, but we hold President Lincoln, from our Illinois land, close to our hearts as he tries to guide the nation forward. With civil war in this land for over half a year, my deep conviction is taken once again for our good home to be a warm respite for whomever knocks at our door, as more people dare to escape. May our dear country finds its true course. I pray she does find her way and with freedom as her beacon of light.
M. G. R. W.

Sarah sat in silence. She was awed by the words she read from Grace's relative who made her home a haven for many people. She wondered why there was not more written by her about the war itself but assumed it must have been too difficult to take the time to commit to words because she was living through a war in her own country. Or maybe those words were put in another diary that had been lost, like all the lost words of freedom seekers that were never written down because it was not safe to document the workings of the Underground Railroad.

Sarah wondered why this brave woman had taken that risk with the written word. She looked again at the repeated signature:

M. G. R. W.

The delicate initials represented a name unknown to Sarah. So much had been lost in that terrible time of slavery and a civil war because of it. Yet such courage had been shown by so many people in her country of birth. Sarah felt humility because she would be living in the very house that revealed a piece of that profound story and had played one small part in a much greater movement.

While thinking about the history that had transpired before her, she realized the Underground Railroad story, an important part of humanity's history, and the more personal story of the twice stolen house, had much light to offer the world. Sarah hoped both stories would be shared over and over. Those stories needed to be told because the bright light of the 1853 house, even if the home had been stolen for awhile, had continued as a beacon for those in need of such light. This was the true gift of the stolen house of light, as a symbol of hope from the past to the future.

Sarah wondered what would have happened if the house had not been saved. She thought if it had been torn down and not moved, then such hope might have been lost, and the lessons they all had learned might never have happened. Sarah might never have known the depth of Tyler's love. Linnea might not have fully grieved the loss of her husband. Sarah might not have discovered her sense of feeling empowered in the world. Linnea would never have learned she could indeed plan and execute a house move. Linnea might never have found her softer, more intuitive side or the generosity in her heart that motivated her to give her house away. There would not have been the knowledge shared worldwide about the Underground Railroad or house moving. Nor would there have been the global outpouring of empathy or funds for a second house. It otherwise would have been torn down, yet it became an old house gifted to Linnea by the remarkable goodwill of the people of the earth.

Two houses had been saved from the bulldozer. Their history and continuity could now meet the promise of the future. Sarah knew most historians would not have wanted the Underground Railroad house to be relocated because its history was linked to the site as well as to the house, and no historian was ever pleased when a house was altered dramatically. Sarah also knew if the house had not been moved it would have been torn down, never to continue its good will. At least the house had been saved and once again aspired to its call for a higher purpose. All its wood was prevented from being put into the dump, and the integrity of the house and its history were not lost forever. The stolen house of light had indeed fulfilled its promise and would continue to be a center of hope.

29

Seasons to Come

Sarah sat with the tranquility of nature calming her as the diary rested on her lap. Sitting quietly she began to think about the various types of houses created all around the world. For years she had kept faithful images of houses, making collages on paper as her hands softly held those pictures and her heart nurtured a sense of interconnectedness. From multiple magazines she documented all the possible homes and then created a book of images of the types of shelter used worldwide. She remembered those soothing images as she sat, enjoying the quiet of her forest. She then decided to walk back through the woods to her home. While carrying the unique diary at her side, she turned in the direction of the old Underground Railroad house where she would reside for years to come.

As Sarah took strides on her land, a whole series of images from her collages came to her imagination. She could see in her mind's eye mud huts, Victorian mansions, igloos, and images of English cottages with thatched roofs. She envisioned tents in the desert, old stone castles of Europe, and geodesic domes built worldwide. There were old Chicago style apartments as big as a house, white washed homes in the heat of Africa and mobile homes of Oklahoma. She remembered the Anasazi cave dwellings in Colorado and the current tin and cardboard makeshift houses around the world made by people with the industriousness of survival.

Images of houses kept flooding her imagination. Sarah could see pagoda-style homes and Japanese houses with movable walls, or bungalows or city high rise condominiums, and motor homes for senior citizens. She thought of houses built on stilts by the ocean, or riverboat houses, and homes with roof gardens in India. There were twelve-thousand-square foot estates in Southern California, and sugar shacks in Mississippi, a-frames, yurts, grass huts, log cabins, houses made from straw bales, and earth-sheltered homes.

As images of the houses of the earth came to her, she recalled how she first had begun to feel empowered on her journey to discover a house and home to call her own. She now asked the difficult questions. Why was housing not available to all people globally, in her own land of birth and in her land of heritage? Why did she, being from one of the wealthiest nations of the world, experience homelessness during her childhood? Was homelessness more common for people of color? Why were one billion people of the earth, one out of six people worldwide, without adequate housing? Why were more than a hundred million people homeless? Sarah knew it was wrong to blame them, and one hundred million homeless people could hardly be blamed, because the causes were many.

Sarah realized her own good fortune in being given a house for free and she felt immense gratitude — but a home was not enough. She wanted to do something to help others without shelter. The 1853 house itself seemed to call to her and encourage Sarah to help others. She wanted to inspire people so they could learn to take destiny into their hands and to feel empowered to create change, and to find the comfort of a home. The courage of freedom seekers and of those who took risks in their homes on the Underground Railroad seemed to guide her still, as did her new sense of empowerment.

As she walked by trees as her companions, she started thinking about an organization she wanted to start where she could raise funds. Through public speaking about the stolen house and selling books of poetry she would one day write, she planned to help organizations around the globe that assisted people to build homes and find ways to sustain their families. She wanted to educate people in the United States about how well constructed many old homes were, so she could help save American houses full of history and valued resources from the earth. She wanted to teach others about the many issues of house teardowns. Sarah wanted to make a difference.

Sarah had lots of ideas and wanted to discuss them further with Binnie and Leroy. She knew they would have good input and with Linnea, Tyler, and the girls helping, they could do something to give to others. Sarah thought about the curious girls, Julia and Blair, and knew they would be happy to do their part in saving houses and being of service. She knew together they all could help people to have a better life, either in a newly built home or in an old house, relocated or renovated.

Sarah walked back peacefully and with joyful anticipation to her house. She reflected on her life as she strolled past the dappled green tree leaves with early hints of yellow. She saw clearly how she had come round full circle. Once homeless as a child, she was now embraced by a sense of belonging in a home given to her out of love. Her life she knew was a connected circle and she now understood how she was intricately part of all existence. With the presence of God evident to her, it was as if an invisible force was guiding her to remember that life could offer her a home that would nurture her ability to be creative and empowered, and to be of service.

With that awareness vivid in her mind, she arrived at her house. She walked up the steps and opened the sturdy oak door, complete with its oval window and glistening peach rose. As she stood at the opening to her house of light, it seemed a bit of magic was in the wind around her gift of a home, moving through trees and encircling the old house. It felt similar to the wind Sarah remembered from days as a child near the bluffs, when someone would call out for her with caring in their voice. Finally she had her own spot of earth where the wind could come at will and playfully swirl its magic around the house first created in imagination, and then with devotion, a house twice given.

Sarah stepped happily into her private world and carefully placed the diary in a special place on a built-in book shelf. She stood for a moment in awe of the diary and what she had read. Sarah looked forward to sharing it with family and friends, and then with a large community of people, even worldwide, who would want to read the old journal. She walked to the kitchen, which seemed to invite her with its warmth and radiant light. She felt love encircling her home as she observed through wavy glass windows the swaying trees in the woods. Then startled, she heard an unexpected knock on the front door and she went back to answer it. To Sarah's surprise, when she opened her front door, she saw Julia, Blair, Binnie, Leroy, Bill, Kathy, Garret, and Tyler—with a grin on his face.

"You won't believe what Leroy and Binnie found out while researching house moving," Tyler said. He was one for getting to the point.

"How did you all know I was here?" Sarah asked. Linnea then showed herself from behind the group.

"I'd arranged for them to surprise you after I planned to give you the house. I hope it's O.K. and we're not intruding," said Linnea hesitantly, knowing Sarah had asked to be alone.

"It's no intrusion; please come in. I had my walk in the woods." Sarah opened the door, welcoming everyone in. "I'd love to finally have you in our home! Hey, Ty. Hi Julia! Can you believe the house is ours?" Sarah reached down to hug her daughter and then held her husband's hand. She felt a closeness with Tyler that she had not felt for some time.

"We came to celebrate your house. And to tell you what we discovered," Binnie said.

"Everyone seems excited...what is it?" asked Sarah.

"Mommy, there is another whole town that moved!" said Julia.

"So many houses!" Blair added.

"You and Linnea told us about Hibbing, Minnesota — the whole town that moved — about one hundred and eighty structures," Leroy told her. "Well, we discovered Ohio has a town that moved around the same time as Hibbing. This was not because of iron ore like they discovered in Minnesota, but to flooding."

"They moved almost four hundred buildings, Mom!" Julia said, not able to wait any longer to tell her.

"Unbelievable!" Sarah said, smiling at the girls, who were excited.

"Two whole towns have been moved," said Tyler, glad he could join in the enthusiasm. He felt as if he was starting to be part of the group.

"Sarah, I think you're going to enjoy this story," said Garret.

"Can we all go in the kitchen and sit?" asked Sarah. They all gathered in the room full of sunlight and sat at the round oak table. Leroy continued the conversation.

"The story we researched at our library says several American Indians warned a settler doing a survey, late in the 1700s. He was told it flooded where he was planning to build a town. They discouraged him from building there, but he didn't listen. The American Indians had been around a long time and knew the land," Leroy told her. "And they were right about the floods."

"I'm doing an article about both towns that moved, Hibbing and Osborn," Linnea told Sarah. "Binnie and Leroy shared their information with me when I invited them to come see you, so I've been researching. In Ohio there were a number of towns that flooded during the 1800s, but the worst flood was 1913. So they planned to build a dam and have a flood plain, but Osborn, a town that had not suffered much flood damage, unfortunately was in that flood plain."

"So they moved four hundred structures about three miles right next to a town called Fairfield," said Bill, who had been following Linnea's story for their next newspaper edition. "Much later the towns changed their old names, Fairfield and Osborn, when they merged. It's now called Fairborn, Ohio. It has a historic district with many old homes that were once moved."

"Just like Hibbing, Minnesota, where many of the moved homes are still there with families in them," added Sarah. "I want to go visit Hibbing one day, and now we can add Fairborn to the list of places to see."

"I wonder if any of the houses in Fairborn were part of the Underground Railroad?" asked Kathy. Bill and Garret told her it was a great question, as Ohio had been very active with many homes having been part of the Underground Railroad.

"Well, something else to research," said Binnie. "But before you go gallivanting off, Sarah, can I give you a hug and congratulate you on your new, old house?" At that there were hugs and handshakes, with everyone celebrating the old house in the spirit of new community. Then to everyone's surprise, except Linnea, there at the back door stood Everett.

"Can a house mover come in and show you what I got?"

"Everett!" said Sarah. "Come in, I'm so glad to see you here!"

"Someone told me *somebody* gave you a house," as he smiled at Sarah and Linnea. "I thought I'd check out the old place. And I have pictures for you to see, of the moves in Hibbing and Osborn," he stated, as he spread the black and white, and sepia toned copies of photos on the old oak table. It was another surprise Linnea had planned. There for all to see was the photographic record of the two most remarkable town relocations in history. It was quite an example of the imagination and industriousness of everyday American people.

Everyone was enjoying the old photos and chatting about how great Sarah and Tyler's house looked. As people kept talking, Sarah excused herself and went to retrieve the old diary from the book shelf. She returned to the kitchen crowded with people she loved and who loved her.

"I have something else to show you. Here's the original diary written by Grace's great, great, grandmother. I've read all the passages about the Underground Railroad, they are marked. She was a good writer. Our town is *very* lucky to have this diary," she shared.

Since Leroy and Binnie had already read their copy, they commented on it as others asked questions. Those who had not seen the diary were anxious to know its contents. As the pages were opened they enjoyed looking at the softly faded ink lettering that documented the vital history. Leroy decided to read some passages aloud. While hearing his rich voice with a deep resonance speak the truth of what had happened in that very house, Sarah again slipped out of the room, this time to have a few moments alone just outside her front door. She had so much to process that was changing in her life. They were good changes, but she still needed a bit of time to reflect.

Hearing Leroy's familiar voice while she stood on the front porch, she knew this was just the beginning. She was happy that many other people would one day read the diary. She looked forward to sharing the history of the house with her soon to be expanding circle, nationwide and globally, including Bangladesh and India, where she planned to one day visit. She felt confident that her family and friends would work together to keep the good will history of the house alive, and to make a difference, be it with homelessness, or the preservation of forests, old houses, and the stories of the Underground Railroad. And Sarah felt certain they would keep celebrating house movers and the houses they move.

Sarah took a deep breath and started to imagine Linnea, Blair, Julia, and herself sitting by the trees, blowing dandelion seeds. She envisioned their daughters with full stems of dandelion puffs and all of them watching those little umbrellas of circumstance float up, gentle in the wind. She knew once again they would share eternity filtering into summer.

Given all Sarah had discovered within herself, she finally had come home to live in her house with a noble history. She knew her imagination would nurture her in good ways while living on the land and in the Underground Railroad home. Standing outdoors on the porch by light filled windows, she had intuitions about her house with its strong structure built of forested wood.

Sarah knew three things about the stolen house of light. She knew her house, aligned with qualities she cherished — creativity, empowerment, justice, and love — would be a home as her center point and a gathering place for many people. Sarah knew her house of light would help her, along with her family and friends, to make a positive difference in the world. And Sarah was certain her house with a gifted and remarkable history, a home in harmony with the trees and the wind, would always remain a haven for her, along with the quiet hymns of nature singing the poetry of seasons to come.

The End

Hibbing, Minnesota, had many houses moved because of the presence of iron ore underneath the town, and it still has the largest open pit iron ore mine in the world. www.hibbing.mn.us.

Fairborn, Ohio, evolved from joining and renaming two towns, Osborn and Fairfield. Like Hibbing, Fairborn is a place where many structures were relocated. At Fairborn Heritage Days, the town expert, Allan Routt, shares his unique research on houses moved from Osborn. www.fairbornheritagedays.com.

North Fort Worth, Texas, has a free *House Moving Museum.* Started by a house mover with a collection of house moving equipment and photos, it shows the fascinating history of house moving. 817-439-1999.

Garnett, Kansas, is a small farm town in western Kansas, where the author's great grandfather, George W. Hunley, lived with his wife, Jane Norris Hunley. They had a lovely home that many years later was offered for one dollar, by another owner of the house, if it was moved. Unfortunately it was torn down thirty years before the author's family moved their home. www.historyandersoncoks.org.

Havana, Illinois, in central Illinois, has homes dating prior to the Civil War. Currently held in an old store front are entertaining musical events, at Occasions. Near Havana is Crane Creek, where the author's great grandfather was born. Havener is a fictional town, not to be confused with Havana, Illinois. www.havana.lib.il.us.

Hinsdale, Illinois, is home to *Katherine Legge Memorial Park,* where the house and studio of architect, R. Harold Zook, was moved. www.zookhomeandstudio.org. Also in Hinsdale is Graue Mill, once a stop on the Underground Railroad. www.grauemill.org

Seneca Falls, New York, has the *Women's Rights National Historical Park,* celebrating the first women's rights convention and showing links between women and abolitionism. http://

www.nps.gov/archive/wori/home.htm.

Chittigong (Chittagong) and *Dhaka, Bangladesh,* are two places the author has traveled and lived. Aspects of this interesting culture are in the novel. See the web for more on this delta region.

Sitka, Alaska, is a coastal town located in the heart of the *Tongass National Forest,* and where the *Sitka Conservation Society* helps protect Sitka spruce trees. www. sitkawild.org.

New London, Connecticut, is home to the historic *Nathan Hale School House,* a 235-year-old building that was moved a surprising number of times. In the book*The Stolen House of Light,* there is a trick to this number for readers to discover with a bit of research. www.connecticutsar.org.

House Moving Resources

Moving a House with Preservation in Mind by Peter Paravalos is a comprehensive look at house moving and preservation issues. Other house moving publications are available through libraries.

International Structural Movers Association sponsors a yearly professional conference and publishes an informative magazine. www.iasm.org.

Peter Friesen from Canada was a mover revered by other movers. Abused as a child, he went on to relocate thousands of large structures that were complex moves. A film documents his life and work. www.petethemovie. com.

The Town that Moved is an enjoyable children's book about Hibbing, Minnesota. It is available through inter-library loan.

Underground Railroad Resources

The Underground Railroad in Illinois by Glennette Tilley Turner includes her thirty years of research. Her books for children include *An Apple for Harriet Tubman,* written after interviewing the great niece of Harriet Tubman. www. ugrr-illinois.com.

National Underground Railroad Freedom Center in Cincinnati, Ohio, pays tribute to the people who escaped slavery and to those who assisted them. www. freedomcenter.org.

Incidents in the Life of a Slave Girl by Harriet Ann Jacobs (under the name Linda Brendt) is one of the first slave narratives written by a woman. Available at libraries.

Preservation Resources

Landmarks Illinois helps to preserve historic and architecturally significant Chicago buildings and structures throughout Illinois. www.landmarks.org.

National Trust for Historic Preservation promotes historic preservation and publishes an informative magazine. www.preservationnation.org.

Embodied Energy, referenced in the book, can be accessed on a chart called the Embodied Energy Calculator. www.thegreenestbuilding.org.

Homelessness Resources

Homeless International funds projects and supports networking globally. www.homeless-international.org.

National Alliance to End Homelessness gives a list of "ten essentials" for ending homelessness in America, and provides conferences and a research institute. www. endhomelessness.org.

Chicago Coalition for the Homeless is a dynamic group that does outstanding work both locally and nationally. www.chicagohomeless.org.

To order this book, please send check or money order for $14.95 (plus $4.85 shipping; Illinois residents please add $1.20 sales tax) to River Pearl Press, 44 Ogden #171, Downers Grove, IL 60515; or visit www. thestolenhouseoflight.com.

A percentage of book proceeds will be donated to these non-profits: Jump for Joel, Trees for Life, Sitka Conservation Society, Chicago Coalition for the Homeless, and LemonAid. For more information see: www.thestolenhouseoflight.com.